GOODYEAR & FORMULA ONE

AIR RACING
1967-1995

VOLUME TWO

BY
ROBERT S. HIRSCH

GOODYEAR & FORMULA ONE
AIR RACING
1967-1995
VOLUME TWO

BY
ROBERT S. HIRSCH

First Edition
First Printing
© Copyright 1998, Robert S. Hirsch

ISBN: 1-891118-23-4

Published by
Wind Canyon Publishing, Inc.
P.O. Box 1445
Niceville, FL 32588-1445

Editor: George Jaquith
Layout/Design: Becky Jaquith
Cover Design: Wind Canyon Publishing, Inc. ©1998
Cover Photos: Provided by Robert S. Hirsch

Wind Canyon Publishing, Inc. offers other book titles. Wind Canyon, Inc. offers software applications work related to book publishing, including converting titles to multimedia CD-ROM discs and other computer formats. For further information, including details regarding the submission of manuscripts, contact the above address.

ABOUT THE AUTHOR

Major Robert S. Hirsch (retired) is a well-known aviation writer and creator of racing aircraft scale drawings which have been internationally acclaimed. He retired from the United States Air Force in 1958 after 23 years of service. His military career included the positions of crew chief and aerial engineer on B-18 and B-26 bombers. He was a pilot then test pilot flying 72 different aircraft. Major Hirsch was also an engineering officer.

Upon retirement he returned to California and worked in aerospace engineering on such projects as the B-70, DC-8, Apollo, Space Shuttle and Space Station. He spent six years on the staff of Santa Ana College. Today he spends full time on his favorite hobbies — aviation research, producing scale drawings of racing aircraft and writing about them. He is on the Board of Directors of the American Aviation Historical Society, and is a member of six other aviation societies. He lives with his wife, Maria, in Buena Park, California.

Author's Note

After 21 years of racing the midgets with the 190 cubic inch C-85 (0-190) Continental engine, this engine was dropped from production and the upgraded 0-200 replaced it. Since most parts in both engines were interchangeable, the 190 cubic inch engine could be converted to 0-200 specifications without much expense. Many racers with C-85 engines were upgraded and continued racing for years. This power conversion set the stage for the new designation "Formula One" and later "International Formula One."

These Engines were to be strictly stock with only A.T.C. qualified parts. The inspectors made every possible effort to develop measuring techniques and procedures that would help detect any exotic or expensive modifications during post-races teardowns. As the years passed, Formula One officials permitted more and more concessions to engine builders, primarily in the interests of reliability and more effective ways of cooling the engines at higher rpm's. During the early years of racing, the stock C-85 engines produced about 3,700 rpm's. The 0-200 specs in 1968 not only provided more cubic inches but also higher compression ratios where the engines could be turned up to 4,200 rpm's. These newer engines produced about 135 hp versus about 100 hp with the C-85's. The cooling system had to be completely sealed with smooth inlet to be effective.

1977 was the year of the International Formula One "revolution" where Europe began serious involvement. The aircraft and pilots racing in Europe are not covered in this book, excepting in an instance or two when an American pilot traveled to Europe to compete. The racing aircraft in Europe represent the latest modifications provided by technological improvements, many of which have come from the United States. For example, if the general specs of a Cassutt made sense for reasons of competitiveness and safety in the Unites States, these same considerations would apply outside the U.S.

This book covers the time frame when women began to compete in pylon racing and, as is shown, they demonstrated that gender is not a consideration in air racing.

Speeds continue to increase among the International Formula One aircraft — now in the vicinity of 285 mph using a Cessna 150 type engine.

As with Volume One, this book is only partly about providing a written history of air racing. I have provided as many scale drawings and photographs as were practical in visually showing the developments in this exciting sport. Any satisfaction I may feel in authoring the text, producing the scale drawings and taking the photographs for these two volumes will depend on being able to impart effectively my love and appreciation for air racing and the wonderful people involved in it.

RSH

TABLE OF CONTENTS

THE STORY CONTINUES —

The year 1967 saw air racing well established. Equipment was more reliable and engineering improvements had advanced the aerodynamics of the midgets over the years. There were still many changes which would be made over the next three decades, and there were some tragic accidents resulting in pilot deaths; but racing was becoming safer and spectator interest was continually increasing. There were, of course, "growing pains," but both the pilots and the governing associations were becoming better able to anticipate and resolve problems. Notably, in 1968 the PRPA rescinded the ban on women as pylon race pilots, and since that time the women racing pilots have competed effectively.

Speeds were increasing each year. Racers had to be continually modified, as reflected in the scale drawing section of this book, in order to stay competitive. From the pilots' perspective, the faster speeds brought the need for even greater concentration and awareness of their surroundings. As a racer rounds a pylon, the earth is turned into a lefthand wall and he is pushed down in his seat. The control stick becomes stiff in his hand, and the cockpit has been likened to a noisy bathtub. His attention needs to be focused primarily on the next pylon.

IN 1967—

In 1967 the Texas National Air Races were held at Luck Field on May 12-13, and they were rained out on the 14th. That day was rescheduled to the weekend of 27-28. Nick Jones in his new Cassutt with upturned wingtips had a thinner wing which made it about 15 mph faster but he could not participate. On the afternoon of May 10th, during a 300-mph dive the wings came off his racer. Jones again suffered minor injuries. Even his parachute landing was a bit rough. The racer had picked up an aileron buzz and then wing flutter before disintegration, which gave Nick a little lead in getting out.

Along with the problem of avoiding turbulence, Reno set the rule that forbids passing on the inside. The pilot overtaking another must keep his quarry in sight during the passing. Going for an altitude will lose speed so being down low is preferred when out in front.

IN 1968—

After January 1, 1968 the 190 C.I.D. Goodyear and Continental Motors Trophies race class permitted the use of the stock 0-200 C.I.D. engine. There was a big scramble to make the change by almost all contestants. A new trend was started with the new 0-200 engines and the racers were designated Formula One racers. Some maintained the old C-85 crankcase which had snugly fit into their engine cowls since the 0-200 would not fit. Others made new cowls. Since 1967 there had been extensive modifications of the midget racers and several new racers had been built.

The first air races in 1968 were at Frederick, MD on July 4th. Since the 1967 Reno races there were several new racers completed and most of the others were extensively modified including the new 200 cubic inch engine. Takeoff acceleration would be more rapid and the expected speed increase would be about 15 mph faster. On the time trials of the first run, the records began to fall. *Rivets* was the winner at 224.8 mph. Roy Berry's *Roadrunner* did 203.13 mph the first time it raced. Roy stuck close behind the duel of Falck's *Rivets* and Jim Wilson's *Snoopy* in the heat race. New engines were allowing considerable increases in speed. Five reached speeds of over 200 mph. *Idjits Midget* did over 199 mph.

On August 29 through September 2, 1968, Cleveland held its second air race since 1950. Known as the Cleveland Nationals it was held at

Burke Lakefront Airport which was ideal for air racing. There were fourteen F-1 racers, as they were then called, ready for time trials. Roy Berry was in #3 *Little Toni* that he now owned. There were three new racers in the group.

Bill Falck topped the time trials at 214.29 mph. On the last day, Howard Terrill was vying for first place when his canopy was smashed by a seagull. He landed safely, however the canopy had been torn loose, and it pushed back and hit and dented his helmet. He also had an injury on his hand that required four stitches.

On the finals race Falck barely edged out Bob Downey 215.246 mph to Bob's 215.053 mph. There were more spectators on the outside of the gate than inside. It was speculated that 125,000 people jammed around the airport. Paid attendance was only about 27,000. People watched from boats, car roofs, on top of railroad cars and buildings.

Later in 1968 at the Reno races, due to the higher altitude, only three of the six finalists topped 200 mph. This was the third time they were held at the de-activated Stead Air Force Base. There were thirteen contestants in F-1's. Ray Cote edged out Bill Falck before 20,000 spectators.

In 1969—

By 1969 women were allowed to compete but only one race was flown by a woman which was an all-women's class racing in stockplanes. No international Formula Ones were raced by women until 1970 when Joan Alford raced her husband Jon's *Pogo* and qualified 10th down of 24 at 200.743 mph.

Change is a permanent part of air racing, and although women were late getting started (through no fault of their own) they took to the Formula Ones and the biplane class like ducks take to water.

The Florida National Air Races held at the Executive Airport at Ft. Lauderdale on February 13-16, 1969 had no fewer than seventeen F-1 official entries, but only fifteen actually flew the time trials. The four-day show was sabotaged by heavy rainfall. John Teglar, the Executive Director, squeezed the

show into two days. It was the first major air competition in the southeast in almost 20 years excluding the small meets in Tampa in 1965 and 1966. Of the five race classes only the midgets could trace their history back to the Miami Air Maneuvers. Up to February 1969 there had been 43 sanctioned events held for F-1 racers. Due to the short time left because of the rain, seven were allowed to fly in the heat races. Falck did 231.26 mph in *Rivets*.

The final Championship race was held up by PAR after T-6 pilot Mac McKinney landed wheels up just before the start of the race. The AT-6 was sprayed with foam to prevent fire. Even though it was still daylight, it was after 6 p.m. when the FAA's waiver ended. The Formula One prize money was awarded based on speeds set in earlier heat races.

On April 28 through May 1, the International Aviation Exposition was held at St. Petersburg-Clearwater International Airport in Florida. No sooner had practice flights begun on that Thursday morning, when news swept through the Midget Racers hanger that Bill Stead had gone into Tampa Bay. An eyewitness reported the plane went into the bay at an angle of about 30 degrees at 100 mph and it did not appear to be under control in the dive. A boat quickly reached the scene but rescue efforts were in vain. Stead was pronounced dead at the hospital. Then despite what at first seemed like a spotty organization with a constant shifting of the events, the spectators saw a high quality racing event. The gloom of the tragedy never seriously produced thought of canceling this type of meet. The course had four regular pylons and two decorated rowboats.

On the time trials, Nick Jones sped his Cassutt around averaging 192.72 mph. Bob Downey clocked only 3 mph faster. Then Bill Falck did a lap at 212.77 mph. During a heat race Jim Wilson made a fast and smooth emergency landing after several inches of his propeller broke off on the first lap. There was a 190 C.I.D. Class speed run over a 3-km course with two runs that averaged at 238.685 mph, and Bob Downey did 227.129 mph. The second day's race was won by Wittman at 199 mph.

The St. Louis races were held August 8-10 in excellent weather with a paying attendance of 100,000 with many more spectators watching from outside. The cover charge was $1.00. Thirteen F-1 racers flew the time trials but in only two races with six racers in each. Number 13 on the list was a standby. Ray Cote celebrated his 20th year of racing with 227.848 mph over Falck's 227.368 mph, but the final race was won by Falck at 222.99 mph with Cote right behind at 222.38 mph. Bud Pedigo was fined $50 for cutting in front of Nick Jones on takeoff and also for low flying.

In 1969 the very-much-liked Leo Holliday died in the crash of a racer he was ferrying to Cleveland for a friend. Each new accident hurt.

On Friday, August 29, 1969, on the Labor Day weekend, time trials started at the Cleveland Lakefront Airport. The course was only 2½ miles instead of the PRPA/NAA required three miles. Officials at the airport explained that relocating the pylon from their 1968 placement would be too expensive.

Twelve Formula Ones qualified. Bill Falck was fastest at 216.87 mph. Jim Wilson in *Snoopy* surprised everyone with second fastest at 203.16 mph. One racer there stood out from most of the others that raced there. It was the 21-year old *Bonzo* now sporting the 0-200 C.I.D. It was Steve Wittman's 40th anniversary of appearances at air races. He simply bolted the new engine on his little yellow racer and the next day took off for Cleveland. Ray Cote set a Cleveland record in the time trials of almost 217 mph.

Dissatisfied with uninteresting heats in 1968, they quit the elimination system. After assignment on the first day from the results of the time trials, if any racer in the consolation event turned a higher speed than one in the finals, they would change places on the second day. This was to encourage more competitive races. In one of the few times in air racing history, Jerry Coughlin and Jim Clement, in the second consolation race, were timed at the finish line precisely the same, declaring the race a dead heat. On the final or Championship race all but one topped 200 mph.

At Reno in September seventeen F-1 racers reg-

istered, and sixteen completed the time trials. They were the fastest group of racers to date. It was also the largest group of F-1's together in eighteen years. Ray Cote was fastest at 219.51 mph but eight topped 200 mph. The 211 mph record was broken by several contestants. By this time there were over 50 midget racers on the NAA register. The *Cosmic Wind* piloted by Roy Berry still raced but on the finals did not finish the fourth lap. Roy got about a square foot cut out of his horizontal stabilizer from Jack Jella's *Grey Ghost* prop which suffered a bent and a ripped tip. Jella went on to finish at over 200 mph but was disqualified. Ray Cote in *Shoestring* beat Bill Falck by about six seconds.

Cy Earnhardt and Mary Coats formed the "Interstate Air Race, Inc." with a 1969 exhibition race in Edention, NC. But then in 1970 they staged a two-class race series of F-1's and T-6's held at Wilson, NC on July 25th and 26th. Nine F-1 racers showed up for the competition. The crowds also were small but the event was a success with some great racing.

In 1970—

Then in 1970, after three years of trying, the management of the Cleveland National Air Races gave up. On January 30 at Cleveland it was announced there would be an air show but no races. The date would be September 5-6. Lack of funding was given as the reason. Then the NAR sanctioned the following air races: April 17-19 Ft. Lauderdale, FL; June 17-21 Cape May, NJ; July 3-5 Hamilton, Ontario, Canada; July 10-12 Frederick MD; August 7-9 or 14-16 St. Louis MO; Sept. 15-20 Reno, NV; and May 15-16 Doodad, England (the first major Formula One Race outside the United States).

By 1970 the Formula One field was no longer short of aircraft. They were actually over-supplied and had to plan extensively for races throughout the country. The biggest change occurred from the contestants. Of the thirty-four long-time participants that competed in all race classes, only ten remained active. Twenty-two were at least temporarily inactive. Two had died, and some of the big names now were unknown five years earlier.

One flaw that would be corrected — the NAA using a percentage of the gate to establish race prizes.

During April 16-19, 1970 at Ft. Lauderdale, FL, the Second Annual Florida National Air Races were held at Executive Airport. John Tegler's third try brought a record 25,000 crowd and thirteen F-1 racers. Nick Jones in his #7 Cassutt III M threw a connecting rod out the top of the engine crankcase just after he finished a race and had to set up an emergency landing. Joan Alford flying an Owl Racer #87 *Pogo* had some spectators on their toes when she picked up some of that lap prop wash and for a very short time experienced tail flutter. Jack Lower's #66 *Idjits Midget* was now Chuck Andrews' *Moonshiner*. Wittman, as always, leaped out in front but eventually Falck overtook him. The Air Race Queen kissed every pilot that raced except Joan Alford. On the first heat race Bob Downey beat Bill Falck by about eight-tenths of a second. It was the first time he had beaten Falck since 1964. James P. Strode of Coco Beach, FL flew the first *Shoestring* built from purchased drawings.

On May 29-31 races were scheduled for Fox Field, Lancaster, CA, then on June 18-19 one was planned for Agvaland, MD and then Reno on September 5-11. Other possibilities were Detroit, Palm Springs and Cleveland. At Reno, Jones & Anderson de-souped their *Shoestring* and John Paul Jones did only 156.3 mph to be competitive with the slower planes. The final winner was Bob Porter at 202.14 mph. He got lost on the first lap and fell behind but several laps at 214 mph made up for it.

In 1970 a regional air race was held in July at Wilson, NC, where a small group spent $3,000 on prize money and took in about $4,000, splitting the profits among the race pilots.

In 1970 the NAA introduced a new policy for racing numbers. They had to be on both sides of the fuselage in block letters and in a contrasting color.

They also had to be at least 24 inches high for the Formula Ones, with a minimum leg of 3 inches. However, number designs already on racers could be approved by the Formula One group, provided they could be read easily during a race. Evidently they were not so strict on this down through the years because there are several racers of the 70s, 80s and 90s that did not conform.

In 1994 the technical rules of Formula One racing were revised to include two stand-alone documents. These were *Procedures* and *Technical Rules*. The TR included specifications for new PMA-approved carburetor venturie and roller rocker arms. Rules Committees were set up to oversee compliance. Only standard unmixed fuel from an on-site common source was allowed.

The PRPA started encouraging and assisting regional air races. By 1971 there were about 50 racers flying and another 40 being built in the U.S., Canada and Europe. In 1973 the Reno F-I class Championship race had eight contestants, and all reached speeds of over 200 mph with only a 24.0 mph difference between the first and last place. This means that the 3-mile course had some very close flying groups that battled it out.

On May 15-16, 1970 at Lincoln, CA the second annual Lincoln Air Races were held. 7,000 spectators attended. The National Air Race Group had a close race between a Formula One and a Formula Vee. The Formula One barely won. Then on May 22-23, the first Formula One race by the Eastern Region of the United States Air Racing Association (USARA) was held at the old USAF glider base in Sturgis, KY over a 2½-mile course. Twelve racers showed up. Charles Terry in No. 14 *Beetlebaum* had a forced landing at Evansville, KY and finally arrived via a trailer. Mike Bryant crashed en route from California and was killed. Only 3,000-5,000 spectators watched from paid seats yet thousands more watched from other vantage points.

At Reno in 1970, the twenty-six racers of the Formula One going through qualification were competing for sixteen racing slots, eight per heat, and it was obvious eight were going to be eliminated. With the caliber of aircraft and pilots that came, if one did not reach up to 190 mph or higher, he was not going to make the field. There were ten that topped 200 mph and the slowest of the sixteen reached 190.81 mph. Bill Falck did 231.263 mph for a new record. Joan Alford in #87 placed third in the Silver at 190.107 mph. Ray Cote won the Championship race at 220.071 mph with Bill Falck second at 215.071 mph. Bob Downey now was fifth, beat out by *Ole Blue*. The slowest qualification flight was turned in by David Butler of Los Angeles, CA at 161.194 mph. Tom Cooney wrapped up his #71 *Tomcat* in a cross country forced landing on the way to Reno.

This was the second year that Formula One International Races were held in England with seven participants. American racers such as Cosmic Wind were bought by the British along with packaged plans. The European International Formula One races were monitored by the United States organization, basically for technical reasons. An accident in Britain during May of 1971 resulting in a fatality stood out. A propeller blade on an Owl-type racer separated from the shaft and the engine vibration tore the engine from its mounts. Then engine retention safety cables were required on all U.S. Formula Ones in 1972. Earlier propellers were made of wood because of costs but thinner metal propellers took over until about 1986 when laminated wood and composite material propellers were used.

In 1971 —

In 1971 on May 15-16 the Wilson Air Races were held at the Municipal Airport at Wilson, NC. Eight Formula One racers showed up and a ninth came up on Sunday and raced in the Consolation race. *Boo Ray* #81 qualified fastest at 222.4 mph over the short 2½-mile course. It also won the final. *Ole Blue* #97 was second and *Mother Holiday* #7 was third. Despite inclement weather at Wilson, over 3,500 paid spectators came and plans were laid to hold another in 1972.

On June 2-6, 1971 major air races were staged at Cape May, NJ with a crowd of 40,000. Eleven Formula One midgets qualified. Bill Falck in *Rivets* arrived late but was allowed to race in the Consola-

tion race which he won just cruising. Nick Jones won the Championship race at a slower speed than Bill Falck's win in the Consolation race. Don Davis was rolled over by prop wash and his *Miss Josephine* dipped into tree tops. He had heavy damage to his racer but managed to land. Tom Cooney flew his new R-3 modified Cassutt and got within ten miles of Cape May. Then he lost a propeller blade. The vibration tore the engine mounts and he shut down power and made an approach to a rice field and the plane flipped over on its back. Tom was all right, however his airplane was washed out.

In 1971 Cleveland again made another try at air racing by staging the Formula One World Championship Trophy Cup Race. It was the first time a major event was held only for Formula One racers. Twenty-five Formula One racers were brought in and fifteen were Cassutts. Judy Wagner flew her first race here. Bill Falck was accused in heat 2-A of cutting a pylon and put back to last place. But pylon number 4 was positioned on Lake Erie and pylon judges were not at the base of the pylon. This was a reminder that adequate and positive judging should be a very important consideration when planning an event.

There were about 45,000 spectators at the airport and more than that outside the fences, but after the politicians barged in and took control of airport functions, the races fizzled for the future. There was a gap between 1971 and 1977 at Cleveland, until Jack Dianiska got a Labor Day race going.

The 8th Annual Reno Races were held September 20-26, 1971. Twenty-seven Formula Ones turned out and had to do two laps to average-out qualifying speed. Nineteen qualified over 200 mph, with the fastest being #92 *Rivets* at 232.258 mph. Seven racers were new. The Medallion race was won by Vincent Delvea in #93 *Ricky Rat*. The Silver Consolation race was won by Judy Wagner in #44 *Solution* at 208.86 mph, and the Championship race was won by Ray Cote in *Shoestring* with Bill Falck second. Six of the eight starters were over 200 mph and old #10 *El Bandito* did 193 mph.

In 1972—

1972 saw races at Wilson, NC. with nine Formula One racers qualifying. No new racers, just highly modified oldies. Then the government funded a $10 million trade show called "Transpo 72" with four days of Formula One races. Eleven racers qualified, with Downey in #14 ahead at 231.10 mph. Bob Downey won heat 1-B with Marion Bakers's #80 *Aquarius* right on his tail with a 0.05 mph difference. Downey had engine problems and dropped back to 5th place in the final, which was won by Falck. Thurman Rock had engine problems in *Ole Blue* on the seventh lap and was forced to land. When Downey landed, he found a gaping hole in his crankcase from a broken rod. *Bennetts Magic*, a modified Cassutt owned by Larry Thompson, crashed and killed Hugh Alexander after a collision with Chuck Andrews in *Moonshiner* on the first lap of the Consolation race.

Reno air races were held on September 12-17, 1972. Attendance was about 60,000. Twenty-three Formula Ones showed up, and qualification times for twelve exceeded 200 mph. Five exceeded 220 mph.

Some of the problems that were becoming habitual with this class showed up. *Stinger* #21 had its cylinder heads milled to allow an excess over the 7:1 allowed compression ratio, but used extra gaskets and passed the inspection. Judy Wagner's #44 also had the heads milled to excess where the gaskets could not correct. She was barred from racing for one year.

Jim Stevenson flew his beautiful purple Owl Race *Fang* #11 in from Van Nuys, CA. It placed third in heat 1-A and fifth in the finals. The Championship race start which had been scheduled for 2:30 p.m. was delayed by Bob Hoover's show which lasted 15 minutes more than had been scheduled. With the Formula One engines all started up in anticipation of a 2:30 start, the delay caused the engines to overheat on most racers. Falck's platinum-tipped sparkplugs fouled on lap 2 and he was out of the race. Ray Cote won in #16. Bob Moeller in #81 was second, and Bob Downey in #14 was third. Jim Hoover was so late to get rolling in his #95 Cassutt he was just approaching the scatter pylon at mid-runway when a clutter of racers went scooting by in the opposite direction.

On October 21-23 there was air racing at Point Mugu Naval Air Station. About 150,000 spectators came to watch the event. Thirteen racers were invited but only ten showed up, so the three "no shows" lost their $50 entry fee. The final race was a real show.

In 1973—

From January 16-21, 1973, the Great Miami Air Races held a major meet at the new Tamiani Airport which is 18 miles southwest of Miami. This was the group's first organized race since 1950. Promoter Dusty Burrows had problems with sponsors and the originally-planned $100,000 fell short by almost $35,000. Thirteen Formula One racers showed up with two being brand new Cassutts. The Consolation race was named after Art Chester and the finals were called the Steve Wittman Speed Classic. There also were four heat races.

Reno held its tenth annual National Championship Air Races on September 11-16 drawing a paid attendance of 60,000. Twenty-four Formula One racers qualified from the 11th through the 13th of September, and one arrived too late but was allowed in the Medallion race. Of the 24 racers qualifying, 16 exceeded 200 mph and 6 of them reached over 220 mph. *Rivets* was tops at 235.244 mph and *Boo Ray* was second with 234.273 mph. Ray Cote had a new wing on his *Shoestring* designed by Stockbarger, an engineer in the advanced design section of North American Aircraft Co.

It must be noted that the midget racers do not perform the same at sea level as they do at the 5,000 ft. level at Reno. Although Bill Falck set a time trial record, Ray Cote won the finals and Falck was 4th at 224.159 mph.

In conjunction with the U.S. Navy's 198th birthday, a two-day show with Formula One racing was run on October 13th and 14th in 1973. It was held at the Miramar Naval Air Station between Escondido and San Diego. It drew about 12,000 spectators. Eleven Formula One racers showed up but Eldon Lutz's new Cassutt was disqualified. The pylon placement created "G" loads up to about 6 and some pilots experienced "grey out." Race officials moved the pylons for the second day of racing. All pilots received $292 except for #87 *Pogo* and #55 *Miss Jerry* whose pilots got an additional $146 for an extra show-off race.

Then on October 18-21 the California Air Classic was held at Mojave, CA with an attendance of about 30,000 spectators. Some of the investors backing the race were well known race people. They lost at least $10,000. This time many of the midgets were noticeably absent. The T-6's, biplanes and Unlimiteds were the show. James F. Stevenson of Oxnard, CA won the Silver race at Mojave in both 1973 and 1974.

On October 27th and 28th, the Point Mugu Space Fair had 180,000 spectators. Thirteen Formula One racers participated. Ray Cote put his *Shoestring* off to the side and did announcing for both days.

The Formula One races were considered the second part of the Quaker State Grand Prix since the Miramar Air Show was considered the first half. The military part of the shows was so complete it seemed repetitious even though all were spectacular. Racehorse starts were out for this event due to the terrain and Navy wishes. A handicap system was devised by George Owl and takeoffs were at timed intervals of three seconds.

In 1974—

Ray Cote won the Mojave Gold in 1974. In 1974 Reno saw twenty qualifiers, with Ray Cote fastest at 240.00 mph in *Shoestring* #16. #21 *Stinger* was second at 234.273 mph and Bob Moeller in *Boo-Ray* third at 226.891 mph with Falck in #92 only 0.476 mph behind him. All eight racers in the Championship reached speeds over 218 mph. Cote won the final at 235.411 mph.

A new design by Jim Miller of Marble Falls, TX created the biggest speculation. Absent from air racing competition for over ten years, Jim returned with a very unusual aircraft. His Miller Special J-2 #73 was a somewhat delta racer with a shrouded four-blade pusher propeller. The shroud contained the elevator and rudder control. The racer was formed over a tubular frame with a composite material. Later, Bruce Bohannan's sister ship was constructed the same way. #73 qualified slowest at only 181.818 mph and placed third in the heat race, but dropped out on third lap of the Medallion race with Tim Wilson as pilot.

It did not take long for #73 to shed its shroud controls by 1975. The size of the shroud was reduced and added were a vertical stabilizer and rudder on top of horizontal control surfaces above the shroud. It still retained its tricycle gear arrangement using a retractable nose wheel. #73 qualified at 203.774 mph.

In 1975—

At Reno in 1975 Ray Cote in *Shoestring* set a qualifying record of 241.611 mph and won the final at 227.464 mph. Vince DeLuca in #71 *Little Quickie* was second at 226.543 mph and Bill Falck in *Rivets* was third at 222.406 mph. Marion Baker in his new #20 *Aquarius* modified from his #80 by making a bubble canopy as his cockpit cover did 214.712 mph to fill last place. 1975 saw twenty-five Formula One racers show up.

Reno did not want to recognize the Professional Race Pilots Association as the official sanctioning organization, which caused friction in establishing rules and safety. Lyle Shelton wrote to all PRPA members that the word *sanction* did not appear in the letters of agreement of the RARA and the PRPA. Earlier the PRPA had just assumed race sanctioning functions from the NAA which was just not equipped to handle it.

Judy Wagner was back racing at Mojave, CA and qualified at 228.33 mph. There were twenty-eight planes that came to compete for the races and these little F-1's put on a good show.

The Desert Sportsman Pilots Association of Falcon Field Mesa, AZ put on a Formula One race on April 3-4, 1976. It was put together through the efforts of Bill Bullock, Ray Cote, E. E. Stover and Ken Haas. There were four races, two each day. Only six racers showed up and raced. They all managed to get into all the race events except Jim Miller's *Texas Gem*, which broke a connecting rod. Allen Grazee was the pilot. Lesser known pilots like David Bice, Paul White and Glen Tuttle got into all four races. Each pilot received $350.

On May 15th and 16th Lincoln, CA, 28 miles NW of Sacramento, held an air race show put on by an all-volunteer crew, called Pylon Air Racing Corp. Over 100 volunteers did all the work and put up $25,000 front money. The site was a de-activated World War II triangular training field. There were only four Formula Ones and one F-V that showed up. The Formula Vee flew with the Formula Ones and was only 9 mph slower than Ted Best in his #4 Cassutt in the Championship race. All the Reno classes were raced in 1975 plus a bomber race.

In 1976—

At Sturgis, KY, the Eastern Region of the U.S. Air Racing Association held races on May 22-23, 1976. The site was the ex-World War II Army glider training base in Sturgis, and the effort came from Union County Airport Board Chairman Jerry McKinney and Truman "Pappy" Weaver. Twelve Formula Ones qualified, plus Steve Wittman in his Formula Vee, the *Vee Witt*. He qualified at 154.639 mph which beat a couple of the F-1's. During the Consolation race on the seventh lap Jack Lowers in his #76 *Spirit of 76* Cassutt was preparing to pass John Rowe's Cassutt #77 on a pylon turn when his left wing sliced through the right wing of Rowe's machine. They both lost a wing panel and crashed about 1,000 ft. from the number one pylon, killing both pilots. This was John Rowe's first air race. The pilots, FAA representatives and air race operators decided to go ahead with the next event. Nick Jones in his #7 Cassutt held onto the lead up to lap 9, then blew his engine but nursed it to the end and finished 6th. *Boo Ray* won at 216.867 mph. Marion Baker in his modified #80, now #20, was second at 213.279 mph.

On June 18-20, 1976 the fourth California National Air Races were held at the Mojave Airport. An FAA administered tower was in operation as was a Flight Service Station for planning and weather briefings. The Mojave Formula One races brought thirteen racers. All but one qualified above 205 mph. [One can fairly accurately estimate a racer's top level speed by adding 25 mph to what it averaged on the 2½-mile course.] After winning the finals at Reno eight times, Ray Cote was disqualified and restricted from further racing for some infraction of the stock engine rules. Judy Wagner did 238 mph and qualified second fastest. The Gold Cup race had all the "Who's Who" in Formula One racing.

Also during July 16-18 the French Formula One Grand Prix Air Race was held just outside Marseille, France with a purse of 40,000 francs. There was also one held at Billund, Denmark. An American advisory board was set up to assist.

Absolutely nothing can match the air races for pure excitement and variety all day. To the race pilot, Reno is the pinnacle event of the year. Air Racing is the language spoken there. The old designs and the new come together. E.M. (Matty) Laird, builder of racing biplanes of the thirties was the special guest at Reno that year, 1976. He was honored by the U.S. Air Racing Association. The grandstands had 27,000 spectators for the season.

Ray Cote was not able to race with *Shoestring* following an infraction during a tech inspection at last June's Mojave races. His appeals were disallowed and he finally packed up *Shoestring* and went home early in the week. The eight-time winner had been slapped down hard by the F-1 class decision-makers. Fred Wofford's qualifying speed of 237.362 mph in his *Proud Bird* and Judy Wagner's 237.760 mph set the stage for intense competition. Judy

Wagner became the first woman to top a list of 19 other contestants in the time trials by being second fastest. The USARA June 1977 Newsletter had *Shoestring* up for sale at $25,000 or best offer by Ray Cote of El Cajon, CA. Wofford's bird was disqualified for alleged illegal intake elbows, a quarter inch too short, as quoted by an inspector during Saturday's race. He, too, packed up and went home.

After being so close to winning for so long Vince DeLuca won the Gold race in his *Lil Quickie*. He said he listened to the engine and did not have to look at the airspeed. He just concentrated on the noise and flew the course. He had been plagued with "gremlins" in the engine throughout the week but a last minute change of mags, harness and plugs did the trick for him. Bob Downey in #28 Dan La Lee Williams *Falcon* came in second followed by Bill Falck and Judy Wagner. John Paul Jones won the Silver race on Saturday in *Stinger* at 214.428 mph. Mike Leoning in the *Flying Dutchman* jumped the starter flag and was disqualified.

By the end of 1976 and beginning of 1977 there was internal strife within the USARA. The T-6 and Unlimited classes withdrew from the organization. Then some Formula One members, not happy with rules, quickly made up a new class and called it International Experimental Limited (IXL) which came out of the difference of opinions of rules for the 0-200 engine and what constituted a stock engine. It was also desirable that the Technical Committee inspectors not be competitors. The T-6's and Unlimiteds started up the National Air Race Group (NAG). This group maintained the Formula One rules and eventually became the replacement for the USARA.

In 1976 the first International Formula One race was held in Le Castellet, France at the site of a major Grand Prix auto racetrack. It was billed as the Formula One Grand Prix Air Race. Senator Bill Sullivan of Kentucky took his Cassutt #51 *Anaconda* to France and beat a field of seven British and one French racer. Formula One racing blossomed in Europe in the late 1970s.

Marion Baker died on July, 29, 1976 in a fatal accident on a cross country flight in his *Delta Kitten*, an E.A.A. home-built.

In 1977—

On June 18-19, 1977 Sturgis, KY held its second annual air race under the direction of Truman "Pappy" Weaver and the USARA. It had the Formula Ones, biplanes and Formula Vee classes. The small number of entries in the Vee class and biplanes eliminated the time trials. All of the Formula Ones qualified except Bill Chevalier in his Cassutt #82 *Blue Angel*. He had lost an exhaust stack on a test flight and could not get repairs in time. It was his first race meet. He entered two races but did not complete either. All of the races for Formula Ones produced speeds of no less than 191.898 mph.

After a six year absence and through the efforts of Jack Deaniska and the USARA Formula One championship racing came back to Burke Lakefront Airport for the Cleveland National Air Show on September 3-5, 1977. There were three Marion Baker memorial trophies sponsored by Dianiska. Here for the first time, drag racing was held for Formula One racers. The FAA waiver for F-1 races at Burke included air starts to eliminate race horse starts.

There was much discussion among the pilots on how to perform air starts and it was finally decided they would form up on the pace-plane flown by Don Fairbanks. The speed agreed upon was 130 mph even though Bill Falck objected that it was a little too slow. He wanted 160 mph since 130 mph was too close to his stalling speed for comfort. Falck was the last to take off and after catching the others he was positioned on the inside for the turns. It was apparent he was having difficulty staying in position with the pack and was approaching a stall in each of the turns. As they turned into the homestretch to start the race, *Rivets* stalled and dove into the lake. It did not flip over and spin but just nosed straight down. Falck was just starting to bring the nose up when *Rivets* hit the water at about a 60 degree angle, killing the 30-year veteran pilot. The stall occurred at 300 feet, which was not enough altitude for recovery. One of the true giants and great competitors of air racing was gone.

The rest of the pack did not see the accident and the race went on, but due to the airport location on the shore a crowd of over 100,000 watched in horror. This tragedy ended flying starts and the FAA rescinded the air start system, replacing it with a handicap method much to the dissatisfaction of the spectators. In the instances when races were held on airports that could not accommodate race horse starts the handicap method was used during the 1980s. John Parker won the finals at 226 mph in another *Shoestring*. Since Ray Cote's 242 mph in the 1975 time trials was faster, it seems the engines were not much changed.

On September 16-18, 1977, the fourteenth Reno National Championship Air Race became the longest continuous air racing in history. The midget racers had a $20,000 purse of the $130,000 total.

There were problems at Reno that year and they eliminated the sport biplane events. They negotiated separately with the T-6, Unlimited and IF-1 classes. The new NARA group provided technical inspection of aircraft and engines but they did not have the capability to sanction the races so no official records were established at Reno.

Qualification runs started on Tuesday with thirteen entries. Ray Cote posted 240 mph over the three-mile course. Ernie Prosch blew his engine in *Loki* and landed in the sagebrush which resulted in a damaged wing and landing gear. Bob Downey failed to qualify *Ole Tiger*. Bob Drew had wheel pants and part of a faring tear off and his propeller nicked the runway. He flew *Wild Turkey* without pants and with a new prop. The first IFM class race was held here. Ray Cote blew an engine and ended up in the Silver race which he won placing him, the fastest of the racers, on the line as an alternate.

Mike Loening died in February 1977 flying his Cessna 210 in a mountain crash near Duchesne, UT.

In 1978—

In 1978 at Reno Ray Cote again led the time trials with 240 mph but the finals were canceled due to high winds and bad weather. On December 16th, Ralph Moore of Titusville, FL flew his new *Shoestring* N-540. The construction of this plane had begun in December 1973. This became Bryan Richardson's *Half Fast* #30 N-1180P in the 90s.

Gary E. Green of Yolo, CO in 1978 hauled his Cassutt III M N-533V on a trailer from his garage to the Yolo County Airport for final checks and FAA inspection before flight testing. It was signed off for flight on July 10, 1978 by an FAA inspector. However, it could not get the required 60 hours flown before the 1978 Oshkosh. It was finally accomplished on March 1979. Gary brought it to Oshkosh from the Yolo County Airport were he was awarded the Michael Seymore Memorial Award for best done Cassutt.

In 1979—

In 1979 the Cleveland Air Races at Burke Lakefront Airport were held over the Labor Day weekend. Owners and pilots of 28 Formula One racers from 14 states from California to New Jersey were notified. Twelve of them showed up for time trials. The leader was Bob Moeller of Hollywood, FL in the late Marion Baker's *Boo Ray* averaging 235.938 mph. Don Beck of Reno in his Cassutt *Gnat* was second at 235.808 mph. Third was John Saum of Toledo, OH in his taper wing Cassutt *Therapy* at 225.470 mph. Jim Miller's new pusher *Texas Gem* flew 222.68 mph. Ten of the twelve racers topped 205 mph. Steve Wittman won the Formula Vee race at 166.069 mph which was a little faster than his *Buster* did in winning the 1947 190-cubic inch race. Technical inspections were performed on all racers resulting in the disqualification of one Formula One and one sport biplane.

At Reno in 1979 Ray Cote in *Shoestring* set a new qualification record at 246.014 mph. John Parker in his special #3 did 240.091 mph. They had learned well what they could do to their engines within the new IXL rules.

In 1980—

On May 22, 1980 J. M. Tuszka lost power on the takeoff run of his Cassutt N5JJ at Stevens Point, WI and sustained damage to prop and engine mounts plus other minor airframe damage. Consequently he never raced it.

The 1980 Oshkosh 500 was won by Jerry Coughlin of Baraboo, WI in his sleek blue and white Cassutt N-6765 #75. Steve Wittman was second 31 seconds behind and Chuck Andrews in *Wise Owl* was third until lap 2 when he lost three-quarters of a prop blade and glided to a beautiful rural paved road and landed on it. Of the 17 aircraft that started the race only seven could stay in the race. Four were forced out, two cut pylons, and four used too much fuel. After winning the Baker Competition in 1979 Jerry Coughlin, won the three events and took home $7,500. Ralph Wise in Owl #17 went out on the second lap with prop failure. Bill Matthias was killed testing his machine for the 500.

At Reno, Ray Cote and John Parker did a similar show as the previous year. Ray Cote did 254 mph to qualify and John Parker won the finals at 249.065 mph in *Wild Turkey*. Cote's 254.06 mph was a new record for the course, however his race speed was only 242.961 mph. The Silver race was won by Don Beck at 224.416 mph in #18 Cassutt and the Bronze was won by Carroll Deitz at 215.491 mph. In the Reno 1980 Championship all were above 217 mph. The Silver race had all contestants above 203 mph, and the Bronze second, third and fourth places were above 200 mph. Don Beck entered the #19 Cassutt in the Bronze but did not finish. The old #31 *Wing Wax* and *Miss San Bernardino* was now #9 *Little Niner* flown by Marshall Wells. This midget had been racing for 33 years.

On October 26, 1980 Chuck Andrews flying Paul Musso's Formula One #68 *Real Sporty* set an unofficial speed record for FAI Class C-l-a. He made four passes over the course at Raleigh County Memorial Airport at Beckley, WV, averaging 236.77 mph. The 1981 season for the now-called International Experimental Limited (IXL) and Midgets was similar to the 1980s with Corvallis and San Diego in August, Cleveland in early September, Reno in mid-September, and then San Marcos in October.

This year at Reno, Ray Cote led both the time trials at 245 mph and the finals at 232 mph. A real sadness fell over both race people and spectators when old-timer Bob Downey died in a crash during practice for the IXL races. Here another great pilot died and was lost to us all. It was thought he had a heart attack on the course.

In 1981—

During the 1981 Corvallis, OR Jaycees Aerial Air Expo, the Pacific Northwest Championship Air Races, became the premier attraction with no fewer than 14 top racers qualifying and racing. The winning speed was 240.45 mph by Ray Cote. At Reno Ray won again for the 13th time.

In 1982—

In 1982, the new set of rules called IXL and set in 1981 were withdrawn and superseded by the Goodyear set of rules, going back to the stock concept for the 0-200 Continental engine with only a few modifications allowed. Safety was the consideration with the FAA, not wanting to approve modifications that each crew could come up with. The new name for this class of racers was International Formula Midgets (IFM). Ralph Wise in his Owl #7 *Sorenson Special* was tops in the time trials at 231 mph but Jon Sharp won the finals at Reno in a modified Cassutt #43 *Aero Majic* at 224.522 mph. Ray Cote's plane was plagued with mechanical problems.

In 1983—

In 1983 the new IFM class events saw new names on top when Chuck Wentwort from Hesperia,

CA made a clean sweep in his #69 *Flexi Flyer* at 239.02 mph in both the time trials and finals. The British Champion Steve Thompson came in second. Ray Cote was still not with it this year. Phil Fogg set a 3-km International Record at 263.45 mph in #4 *Aloha*.

In 1984—

At Reno in 1984 Ray Cote was back and dominated the events in the former Judy Wagner's #44 *Solution*. The IFM class had six heat races plus the Bronze, Silver and Gold Cups and seemed to get back on track a little over the 1983 doldrums. Ray Cote led the qualification times with 238.568 mph. Twenty-two racers qualified and most of them got to race somewhere on the list.

The Gold Cup race was won by Cote at 236.07 mph or about 3 mph slower than the 1983 win by Chuck Wentworth. Tom Aslett in Eldon Lutz's designed *Flying Dutchman* #38 was not far behind at 235.344 mph. Former 1982 champion Jon Sharp was third in his *Aero Majic* at 233.812 mph. Jim Miller in his delta-type pusher *Texas Gem* was fifth right behind Dusty Dowd in *Illusion*. Don Beck was sixth in *Miss USA* and Jim Harris was an added starter having won the Silver Cup. Chuck Andrews lost his life the week prior to the Reno event testing his #66 *Moonshiner*.

In 1985—

In 1985 the typical IFM racer entry at Reno was the Cassutt and mods of it. But *Shoestring, Flying Dutchman,* Miller's *Texas Gem* and *Alouette* were very much in competition. It was Ray Cote winning again in both — time trials at 241 mph and 229 mph in the finals. Gary Hubler failed to start in the Bronze race and his Cassutt *Black Majic* was promptly loaded on his trailer for a trip back to Caldwell, Idaho. Deke Slayton and Lori Love, the only woman in the race, swapped second and third places during the Silver race but Love finally moved out and took second place.

Jon Sharp was a favorite but a balky engine prevented starting in heat 2-A and a wrong turn in heat 1-A cost him his lead and so he did not get into the Gold. His 230.513 mph in the Bronze was faster than Ray Cote's Gold win.

In 1986—

1986 was the twentieth anniversary of the Reno races held at Stead Field. The USARA also held races at Detroit, MI August 9-10; Columbus, OH August 23-24; and Cleveland, OH August 30 through September 1. The Reno event was held September 11-14 so these little midget racers really got moved around to compete in all of these events. Some did not. Then also, the NAG held one on August 16-17 at Richland, WA. At Reno Jon Sharp's Cassutt #43 won both speed honors, 241 mph on time trials and the Gold Cup Race at 230 mph. Kirk Hanna in #7 *Wise Owl* set a 15-km record of 247.65 mph.

Jeff Sawyer of El Cajon, CA. was killed August 23, 1987 while flight testing a new F-1 he had planned to enter in the Reno races. He had flown the Owl *Lucy P* at Reno in 1985 and 1986. The DF-9 of Sawyer's was designed by Doug Fronius. It had a 27 ft. Owl wing, a long narrow fuselage and T-tail. The accident occurred at the Ramona Airport on the DF-9's third test flight when Jeff made a high speed pass, and part of the elevator separated. The plane had been designed and built in ten months.

In 1987—

At Reno in 1987 Alan Preston piloted Judy Wagner's *Shoestring*. It held the top speed during the qualification trials at 241.189 mph, then took heat 1-A at 232.838 mph. James Miller was fourth down on the time trials with 226.136 mph but placed second in the race in his new *Pushy Cat* #14 at 230.6012 mph. Miller, in his new pusher, crossed the finish line of the finals ahead of Preston but was penalized for cutting a pylon. *Pushy Cat* was constructed of a composite skinned tubular frame aircraft.

Since Bill Stead got the Reno races started 29 years earlier, there have been many different races flown there with many different pilots covering thousands of miles. Of the 22 IFM racers to qualify that year, 18 of them reached over 200 mph and only one was below 194 mph.

In 1988—

1988 was the twenty-fifth anniversary of Reno's air racing, but one of its contestants was missing. Sixty-five year old retired USAF Col. Bill Skliar of Reno was killed August 18th. He was testing *Shark* #41 when the right section of its new wing broke off in flight. Then Robin Reed nearly crashed in #85 *Super Skate* when the prop came apart. He got it down on runway 32 but damaged his gear in an overrun. Ray Cote did his practice flights in Kathy Grey's #87 to qualify her aircraft for her. There were 23 racers qualified and by August there had been 29 that had signed up. Jim Miller put a new prop and extended shaft on his seatless *Pushey Cat*. Jim sat on the floor, all for lightness. In just about all the heats, the first four places were the same. First was Alan Preston in Wagner's #44. Second was Miller close behind in #14. Third was Jon Sharp in #43 *Aero Majic*. Cote was fourth in *Alley Cat*. Miller had to pull out of the Gold race with mechanical problems, which put Jon Sharp in second. The highest speed attained was 237.814 mph. Ray Cote won the Silver Cup in *Alley Cat*. John Dowd won the Silver heat F-1 in #77 *Super Spook* and Jim Harris took the Bronze in #25 *Gold Fever*. The Formula One racing circuit had been growing in numbers of pilots and racers each year.

In 1989—

On Sunday, August 20, 1989, Ray Cote attempted to break the 261 mph speed record at Wichita, KS but threw a rod on his third pass and could not get repairs completed in time to continue. At Reno in September Jon Sharp was at the controls of the Boyd GR-7, #96 *Blue Streak* and put up the fastest qualification time at 242.548 mph. *Blue Streak* was constructed of all composite material without an internal framework. Ray Cote in #4 *Alley Cat* was only three-tenths of a second behind him. Jim Miller was third at 238.975 mph and the second GR-7 (#55) with Jim Buford was fourth at 237.103 mph. "Hoot" Gibson, the NASA Astronaut in his #92 *Poly-Dynamite*, placed 5th at 198.599 mph. He was second in heat 2-C on Friday at 196.197 mph. Ray Cote won again in the Gold with #4 *Alley Cat*.

In heat 1-A Miller's *Pushy Cat* beat Sharp in *Blue Streak* by 7.435 mph. In the Gold Cup race Sharp in #96 did not finish. There were 28 entrants for the 24 slots selected from the time trials. [The qualifying speeds posted determine the starting positions and what heats they will race in. They, in turn, determine the starting positions and who will participate for the finals. The qualifying runs consist of two to four practice runs followed by one officially-timed run. Each pilot is permitted to qualify only once and can be assigned only on the qualifying time.] The fastest eight flew in the 1-A race. The next seven (9 through 16) went to the 1-B race and 17 through 24 went to 1-C and the Consolation race.

In 1990—

In 1990 at Reno, no fewer than 29 midget racers signed up for the IFM class. Some of the new ones were Bruce Bohannon's *Pushey Galore*, a copy of Jim Miller's *Pusher*. Bruce qualified at 215.806 mph. It did 211.116 mph in Friday's heat 2-A race. Another racer was the second GR-7, designed by Robby Grove and flown by Jim Bumford, and was named *Bummers Bullet*. It qualified at 228.817 mph. Dave Morss of San Carlos, CA, with his large span tandem wheel race placed second in heat 1-C at 199.115 mph. Dave qualified the same racer at 205.62 mph.

Jim Miller won heat 2-A at 230.187 mph and Ray Cote won heat 2-C at 225.845 mph. Then Miller won the Gold on Sunday at 237.548 mph. On his tail and only 0.321 mph behind him at the finish line was Hep Porter in #44 *Shoestring* at 237.084 mph. Jim Bumford was third in *Bummers Bullet* at 233.874 mph.

In 1991—

The year 1991 belonged to Jon Sharp of Lancaster, CA. He came with his Sharp DR-90 named *Nemesis* which was a new design of all composite material but appeared to be a redesigned *Shoestring*. The DR-90 was designed by Jon Sharp and Steve Erickson. There were 27 entries trying for the 24 slots on the bill. This year Jon raced for his fourth championship. He won at a speed of 245.264 mph. William Ippolito of Long Beach, CA won heat 2-B at 233.749 mph. Katherine Gray from Santa Paula, CA, racing for the fifth year placed third in heat 2-B in her Owl OR65-3 *Pogo* at 214.324 mph. Also Madeline Kenny of San Carlos, CA, racing for her second year in her Cassutt II M *Fandango* #41 placed third in heat 2-C at 185.382 mph. Of the "old" racers only Budde's #10 *El Bandito* was still in there trying.

In 1992—

There were only twenty-three IFM Midgets that qualified in 1992 at Reno between Monday and Thursday, leaving one opening not filled. Jim Bumford qualified the fastest at 252.788 mph with Jon Sharp second at 249.743 mph. Miller was third at 242.128 mph. Hep Porter was now flying Wagner's #44 *Shoestring* and was fourth at 238.416 mph. Jon Sharp won the Gold again at 238.175 and Porter was second at 232.306 mph. Jim Miller was third at 231.012 mph, and between the two Miller-designed pushers #14 and #89. Bumford did something wrong to his engine because he was fourth at only 227.787 mph, 25 mph below his time trial. Scott Morris won the Silver in his Cassutt #33 *Sahara* at 215.619 mph which was also 10 mph below his time trial. The Formula One midgets were now flying faster on the 3-mile course than the AT-6's on the 5-mile course. Maybe the Formula Ones should also be on the 5-mile course to incur lower G forces.

In 1993—

By 1993 almost all the racers at Reno were the basic designs of *Shoestring* or Cassutts. The Cassutts had been the greatest in numbers with *Shoestrings* second. Almost all had been modified to where they hardly could be related to the original design. Miller's first pusher had been modified many times but was destroyed earlier in a crash due to a desert dust devil. His other two, Nos. 14 and 89, had very few changes. The two GR-7 models were not modified in configuration since they were constructed of all composite foam materials.

Bobby Budde qualified his *El Bandito* at 222.452 mph. George Budde qualified his *Okie Stroker* at 204.892 mph but did not get his #19 *Okie Streaker* qualified. Jon Sharp in *Nemesis* qualified at 254.223 mph and won the Gold at 250.703 mph. Jim Miller was second at 242.01 mph. He had qualified at 248.358 mph. Alberto Rossi in his Cassutt *Chico Puro* #63 was third at 236.785 mph and Bruce Bohannon was fourth at 234.503 mph. Kathy Gray was an alternate pilot for #95 *Mariah* which Gary Hubler flew to 5th place in the Gold, and Madeline Kenny was again in #41 and placed second in heat 1-C on Thursday.

In 1994—

During June 4-5, 1994 Paso Robles, CA held IFM races and again Jon Sharp qualified the highest at 254.81 mph out of a field of fifteen starters. All but two topped 200 mph to qualify. There were six races and Jon won the final at 243.84 mph. Bruce Bohannon landed with his nose gear up but damage was minimal. He was at the Reno races that year with his new wingtips and air scoop.

There were 27 entries at Reno and three would be eliminated. Bryan Richardson of Auburn, CA had the prettiest but not the fastest Shoestring K-10, #30 *Half Fast*. In 1990 he qualified at 183.421 mph and this year he did 209.97 mph. Dave Morss did not qualify his #99 for the first time since 1990. This was Reno's 30th anniversary of racing and 47 years for the midgets.

The Gold Race was not much of a contest with Jon Sharp about 10 mph ahead of his nearest competitor. Jon's speed was 242.857 mph and Jim Miller running second flew in at 232.9 78 mph. Gary Hubler in #95 was third at 225.652 mph, and Katherine Gray in #96, the GR-7, was fifth at 221.188 mph right on the tail of Dave Morss in #92 (a modified "Hoot" Gibson's *Poly-Dynamite*) at 221.330 mph.

The near mid-air collision between two midgets landing during qualification trials helped motivate the FAA and the International Formula One people to talk about mandatory radios. They were used quite effectively during pre-racing flight checks. Radios became a requirement for the 1996 events.

In 1995—

On March 24-26, 1995 the second annual Phoenix 500 was held in Arizona. Jon Sharp won with his famous Nemesis at 249.904 mph. Then on May 5-7 races were held at Cleveland, and on September 14-17 the 32nd annual NAR were held with no fewer than 27 racers showing up to race at Reno. Again, Jon Sharp in Nemesis won the Gold at 250.268 mph.

Between races, owners and pilots go back to their shops and drawing boards to work at making their little racers faster. Even a small change can bring about a big surprise to competitors in the next races.

A standard procedure for pilots who race for owners is that they get 40% of the purse. It certainly is not a money-making activity. The pilot/owner must cover all expenses of his crew and pay for their time since they are not the gamblers for the shares of the purse. But when he gets top money he always provides a bonus for the crew.

There were differences of opinion among the competitors on how to ferry their racers to the competition. Some came on trailers and with their mechanics, and some flew to the scene. Steve Wittman always flew his racer to the scene and did all the work himself rather than bringing a mechanic. Mechanical problems plagued all the competition pilots and owners at one time or another.

Racing is both a hobby and hard work, and pilots have to keep trim. The average age of Formula One pilots today in the mid 1990s is about 47½ years. Each pilot is issued a valid Formula One racing pilot's license when he/she meets the qualification requirements.

At air races like Reno, many fans have the same seats each year and there is a kinship that develops in the grandstands. Friendships evolve from just sitting next to each other. Almost every race fan develops a family of friends. One group of enthusiasts at Reno grew numerous enough to reserve a large section in the grandstands. They put up a banner and canopy, and also wear custom made tee shirts and hats for identification. Fans come from all over the country. They have nothing in common except that they meet each year at the races. The majority of these fans fit the air races into their vacation allowance.

As far as the participants are concerned, they love everything about racing. One problem with IFM racing today, as it has gained in popularity, is logistics. Not everyone can take off from a job or work for 10 to 14 days two or three times a year to drive to wherever a race is to be held. In addition it is expensive to haul a trailer with a plane and equipment across the country. Each race crew must plan and juggle their activities during the racing season in an effort to compete in as many races as possible. It is not uncommon for a racing team to travel 20,000 miles in a year.

These IFM pilots are true descendants of the "backyard" racers of the 1930s. To many of them, racing is irresistible. As 1997 marked the 50th anniversary of their little midget racers, it seems certain that these men and women will continue to entertain and thrill fans well into the future.

GOODYEAR & FORMULA ONE WINNERS

Year	Where	Pilot	Race #	Racer	Speed (MPH)
1947	Cleveland, OH	Bill Brennand	20	Buster	165.857
1948	Miami, FL	Bill Brennand	1	Bonzo	166.473
1948	Cleveland, OH	H. (Fish) Salmon	4	Minnow	169.668
1949	Miami, FL	Steve Wittman	1	Bonzo	176.867
1949	Cleveland, OH	Bill Brennand	20	Buster	177.34
1949	San Diego, CA	H. (Fish) Salmon	4	Minnow	175.27
1949	Newhall, CA	Bob Downey	4	Minnow	169.4
1949	Ontario, CA	Bob Downey	4	Minnow	176.0
1950	Miami, FL	Steve Wittman	1	Bonzo	185.4
1950	Detroit, MI	John Paul Jones	3	Little Toni	187.785
1950	White Plaines, NY	Bill Brennand	20	Buster	1.75.47
1950	San Jose, CA	Vincent Ast	16	Shoestring	1.75.0
1950	Chattanooga, TN	Bill Brennand	20	Buster	1.76.69
1950	Reading, PA	Steve Wittman	1	Bonzo	1.85.57
1951	Detroit, MI	John Paul Jones	16	Shoestring	197.218
1951	Chattanooga, TN	Steve Wittman	1	Bonzo	178.36
1951	Reading, PA	Steve Wittman	1	Bonzo	184.69
1952	Detroit, MI	Steve Wittman	1	Bonzo	197.29
1952	Chattanooga, TN	Bill Falck	92	Rivets	186.95
1954	Dansville, NY	Jim Miller	14	Little Gem	181.06
1955	Dansville, NY	Bill Falck	92	Rivets	186.85
1956	Springfield, IL	Bill Falck	92	Rivets	191.07
1956	Niagara Falls, NY	Bill Falck	92	Rivets	199.96
1956	Oshkosh, WI	Steve Wittman	1	Bonzo	196.84
1957	Oshkosh, WI	Steve Wittman	1	Bonzo	192.76
1957	Ft. Wayne, IN	Bill Falck	92	Rivets	196.65
1958	Fulton, NY	Bill Falck	92	Rivets	196.72
1958	Ft. Wayne, IN	Tom Cassutt	111	Cassutt Special	195.8
1959	Ft. Wayne, IN	Jim Miller	14	Little Gem	199.15
1960	Ft. Wayne, IN	Jim Miller	14	Little Gem	200.23
1964	Reno, NV	Bob Porter	14	Little Gem	193.44
1965	St. Petersburg, FL	Bill Falck	92	Rivets	200.75
1965	Las Vegas, NV	Bob Porter	39	Deerfly	202.4
1965	Lancaster, CA	Bob Downey	14	Little Gem	195.0
1965	Reno, NV	Bob Porter	39	Deerfly	202.14
1965	Palm Springs, CA	John Paul Jones	16	Shoestring	202.17
1966	St. Petersburg, FL	Bill Falck	92	Rivets	203.01
1966	Lancaster, CA	Bob Downey	14	Ole Tiger	189.48
1966	Frederick, MD	Bill Falck	92	Rivets	192.8
1966	Reno, NV	Bill Falck	92	Rivets	193.098
1967	Ft.Worth, TX	Bill Falck	92	Rivets	203.97
1967	Cleveland, OH	Bill Falck	92	Rivets	202.893
1967	Reno, NV	Bill Falck	92	Rivets	202.703
1968	Frederick, MD	Bill Falck	92	Rivets	218.18
1968	Cleveland, OH	Bill Falck	92	Rivets	215.246
1968	Reno, NV	Ray Cote	16	Shoestring	214.605
1969	St. Louis, MD	Bill Falck	92	Rivets	222.99
1969	Ft. Lauderdale, FL	Bill Falck	92	Rivets	231.26
1969	Reno, NV	Ray Cote	16	Shoestring	225.548

GOODYEAR & FORMULA ONE WINNERS

Year	Where	Pilot	Race #	Racer	Speed (MPH)
1970	Ft. Lauderdale, FL	Bill Falck	92	Rivets	210.91
1970	Wilson, NC	Bill Falck	92	Rivets	210.0
1970	Reno, NV	Ray Cote	16	Shoestring	224.14
1971	Cleveland, OH	Bill Falck	92	Rivets	213.02
1971	Cape May, NJ	Bob Moeller	81	Boo Ray	214.70
1971	Wilson, NC	Bob Moeller	81	Boo Ray	220.20
1971	Reno, NV	Ray Cote	16	Shoestring	224.14
1972	Wilson, NC	Bob Downey	14	Ole Tiger	214.692
1972	Washington, D.C.	Bill Falck	92	Rivets	227.20
1972	Point Mugu, CA	Bob Downey	14	Ole Tiger	213.0
1972	Reno, NV	Ray Cote	16	Shoestring	223.95
1973	Miramar NAS, CA	Ray Cote	16	Shoestring	249.5
1973	Point Mugu, CA	Vince DeLuca	71	Lil Quickie	221.1
1973	Reno, NV	Ray Cote	26	Shoestring	231.263
1973	Miami, FL	Bill Falck	92	Rivets	224.53
1974	Evansville, IA	Nick Jones	7	Mother Holiday	214.797
1974	Mojave, CA	Ray Cote	16	Shoestring	221.444
1974	Reno, NV	Ray Cote	16	Shoestring	235.422
1975	Mojave, CA	Ray Cote	16	Shoestring	231.88
1975	Flora, IL	Marion Baker	20	Aquarius	208.456
1975	Reno, NV	Ray Cote	16	Shoestring	227.46
1976	Mojave, CA	Fred Wofford	9	Proud Bird	237.362
1976	Sturgis, KY	Bob Moeller	81	Boo Ray	216.867
1976	Reno, NV	Vince DeLuca	71	Lil Quickie	228.75
1977	Cleveland, OH	Bob Moeller	81	Boo Ray	224.06
1977	Reno, NV	John Parker	93	Top Turkey	226.12
1978	Mexicali, Mexico	Bill Skliar	41	Shark	210.31
1978	Oshkosh, WI	Steve Wittman	1	Bonzo	196.0
1978	Cleveland, OH	Jim Miller	73	Texas Gem	233.26
1978	Reno, NV	NO FINAL RACE DUE TO RAIN AND WIND			
1978	Mexicali, Mexico	Don Beck	18	Gnat	217.26
1979	Reno, NV	John Parker	3	Wild Turkey	240.09
1979	San Diego, CA	Ray Cote	16	Shoestring	237.026
1979	Cleveland, OH	Bob Moeller	81	Boo Ray	223.002
1980	San Marcos, TX	Judy Wagner	44	Wagner Solution	232
1980	San Diego, CA	Ray Cote	16	Shoestring	233
1980	Cleveland, OH	Bob Anspach	93	Pole Cat	233.88
1980	Reno, NV	John Parker	3	American Special	249.07
1981	Corvallis, OR	Ray Cote	16	Shoestring	224.95
1981	Reno, NV	Ray Cote	16	Shoestring	232.13
1982	Petersburg, VA	Jim Miller	73	Texas Gem	223.064
1982	Reno, NV	Jon Sharp	43	Aero Majic	224.52
1983	Beckley, WV	Jim Miller	73	Texas Gem	210.321
1983	Reno, NV	Chuck Wentworth	69	Flexi-Flyer	239.02
1984	Columbus, OH	Chuck Andrews	68	Real Sporty	194.245
1984	Reno, NV	Ray Cote	44	Judy	236.07
1985	Reno, NV	Ray Cote	44	Judy	229.09
1985	Cleveland, OH	Jim Miller	73	Texas Gem	220.97
1986	Reno, NV	Jon Sharp	43	Aero Majic	229.614

GOODYEAR & FORMULA ONE WINNERS

Year	Where	Pilot	Race #	Racer	Speed (MPH)
1986	Richland, WA	Alan Preston	44	Sitting Duck	234.227
1987	Reno, NV	Alan Preston	44	Judy's Sitting Duck	232.989
1988	Reno, NV	Alan Preston	44	Sitting Duck	240.748
1988	Waco, TX	Bill Skiiar	18	Miss USA	210.16
1988	Albuquerque, NM	Jim Miller	14	Pushy Cat	232.19
1989	Reno, NV	Ray Cote	4	Alley Cat OR-71	231.251
1989	Cleveland, OH	Jim Miller	14	Pushy Cat	183.556
1990	Reno, NV	Jim Miller	14	Pushy Cat	237.405
1991	Reno, NV	Jon Sharp	3	Nemesis	245.264
1992	Reno, NV	Jon Sharp	3	Nemesis	238.175
1993	Reno, NV	Jon Sharp	3	Nemesis	255.257
1994	Phoenix, AZ	Jon Sharp	3	Nemesis	244.349
1994	Reno, NV	Jon Sharp	3	Nemesis	248.911
1995	Phoenix, AZ	Jon Sharp	3	Nemesis	250.268
1995	Reno, NV	Jon Sharp	3	Nemesis	249.904
1995	Cleveland, OH	Jim Miller	73	Texas Gem	220.97

RENO 1996 ENTRY SEPTEMBER FORMULA FORUM —

Race No.	Registration	Name	Type	Owner
2	N8EW	Okie Swinger	Wagner	Budde B.
3	N18JS	Nemesis	Sharp	Sharp
4	NIVD	Alley Cat	Owl	Cote
6	N102	Okie Stroker	Cassutt	Budde G.
10	N16G	El Bandito	Cathaway	Budde B.
11	N25VS	Frenzy	Cassutt	Hoover
14	N414M	Pushy Cat	Miller	Miller
17	N45689	Annie	Cassutt	Swenson
19	N119	Okie Streaker	Cassutt	Budde G.
24	N24ML	Spud Runner	Shoestring	Rediker
27	N227RS I	Silver BB	Cassutt	Kuenzi
29	N29PS	Baby Dragon	Cassutt	Nusz
36	N236PS	Firefly	Kelly FID	Myers
38	N38Z	Flying Dutchman	Lutz LFD4	Maslen
39	N390DG	Shadow	Sharp	Gilbert
40	N5381	Miss USA	Cassutt	Johnson
42	N100K	Barbara Jean 2	Kelly	Kelly
43	N14SJ	Aero Majic	Cassutt	Housley
44	N44JW	Judy	Shoestring	Hauptman
57	N603R	Knotty Boy	Cassutt	Sherwood
63	N63CP	Chico Puro	Cassutt+	Rossi
69	N55X	Miss Reno	Cassutt	Kikkert
89	N189BB	Pushy Galore	Miller	Bohannon
92	N17517	Yellow Peril	Cassutt	Matheson
95	N11XR	Mariah	Cassutt	Hubler
96	N687RB	Madder Max 1	Grove	Howell
99	N799DM	Sahara	Cassutt	Morss

THE AIRCRAFT

1982-85
"Sundowner"
"Alouette"

The "Sundowner" is a modified "Shoestring" built by Schultz-Wagner. It raced at Reno from 1982-85. The pilot was Robert Drew of Los Gatos, CA. It was called "Friberg Electric" in 1985-87. George L. Budde of Midwest City, OK brought it to Reno from 1990-1994. It was flown by Bobby M. and George Budde. Its fastest qualification speed was 225.644 mph. At one time it was named "Alouette."

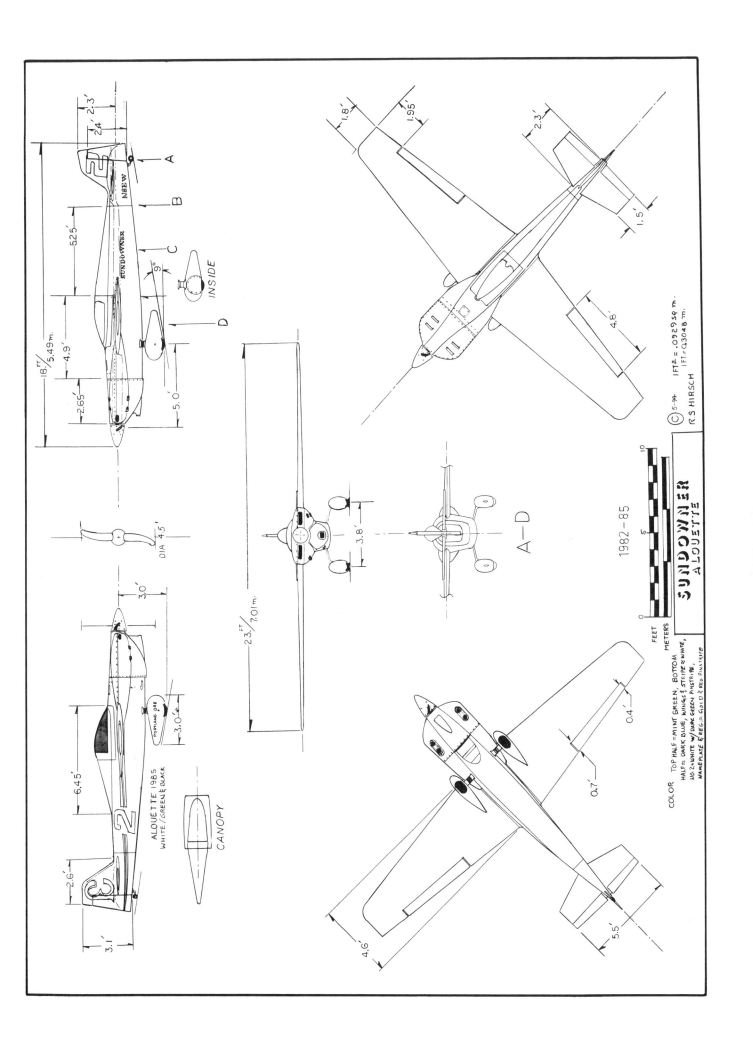

SUNDOWNER
ALOUETTE

1982-85

FEET
METERS

© 5-94 1FT² = .0929 SQ m.
R S HIRSCH 1FT = 0.3048 m.

COLOR TOP HALF = MINT GREEN, BOTTOM
HALF = DARK BLUE, WINGS + STRIPE = WHITE,
NO. 2 = WHITE w/ DARK GREEN PINSTRIPE,
NAMEPLATE & REG = GOLD & RED PINSTRIPE

A – D

INSIDE

CANOPY

ALOUETTE 1985
WHITE / GREEN & BLACK

DIA 4.5'

N8EW
SUNDOWNER

1976-78
"WILD TURKEY"
JP-001

The JP-001 "Wild Turkey" came on the scene at Reno in 1976. It was built by John Parker of Torrance, CA. The wing plan form was so unique it was almost disqualified. The pilot was Bob Drewat in the 1976 races. John Parker won his first Gold Cup race at 245.329 mph in 1977, and his second win came in 1979 at 249.065 mph. It was also named "American Air Racing Special." It was designed by John Cook, an Englishman. It had wheel pants problems in 1977-78.

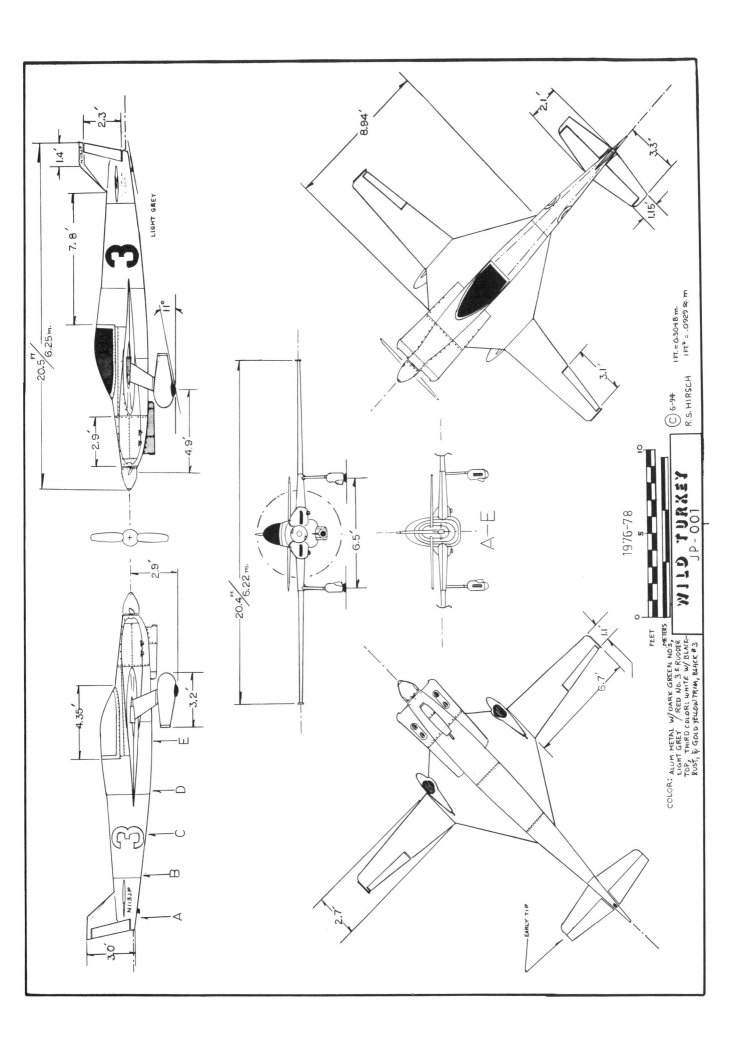

LIGHT GREY

N113JP

3

2.3'
1.4'
7.8'
20.5' FT / 6.25 m.
2.9'
4.9'
11°

2.9'
4.35'
3.2'
20.4' FT / 6.22 m.

A B C D E

N113JP
3
3.0'

6.5'

A-E

8.94'
2.1'
3.3'
1.15'
3.1'

EARLY TIP
2.7'
6.7'
1.1'

1976-78

WILD TURKEY
JP-001

COLOR: ALUM. METAL W/ DARK GREEN NO'S,
LIGHT GREY RED NO. 3 & RUDDER
TOP, THIRD COLOR: WHITE W/ BLACK-
RUST, & GOLD YELLOW TRIM, BLACK #3

1 FT. = 0.3048 m.
1 FT² = .0929 sq. m.

© 6-94
R.S. HIRSCH

10

5

0
FEET METERS

1991
JON SHARP
TECH MACHINE

Jon Sharp's DR-90 Tech Machine called "Nemesis" appears to be a highly modified "Shoestring." John is from Lancaster, CA. The DR-90 set a new class record of 260.916 mph at the Phoenix 500 in 1995, and won the Gold race with 250.268 mph, lapping two other contestants. It made a name for itself as the winner of the 1992 Air Races in Reno. His racer has the right combination of engine and propeller for the 290 mph speed range. Jon has won all big races and finals in this since 1992. It's a guess on how much longer he can win everything.

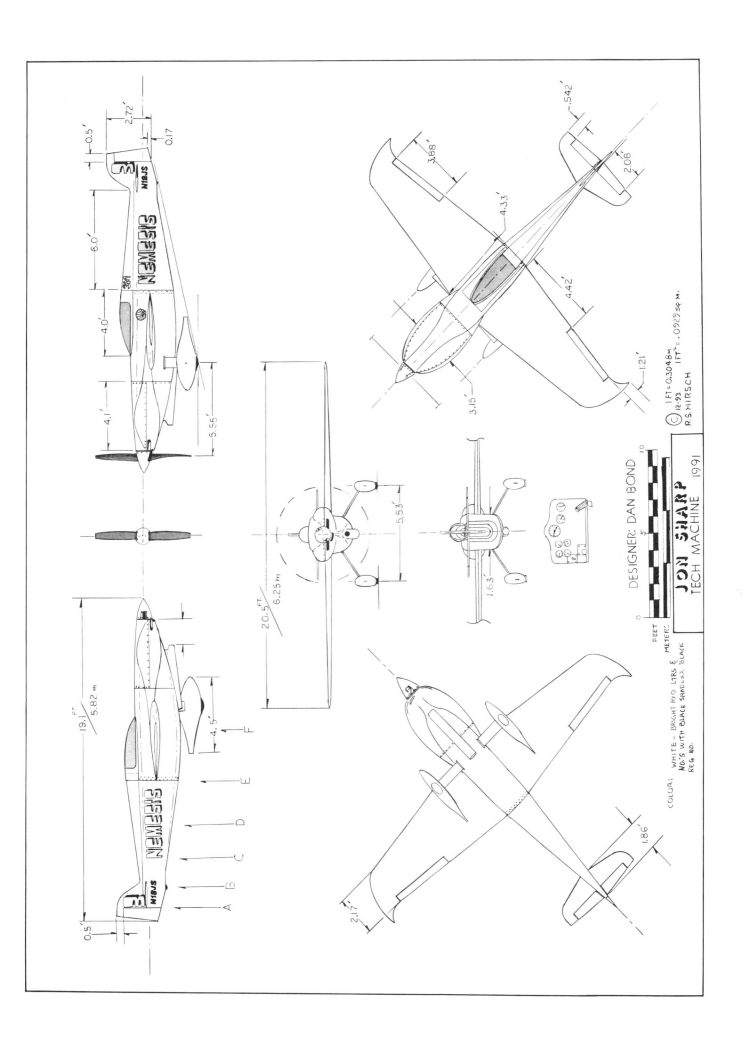

NEMESIS

N18JS

DESIGNER: DAN BOND

JON SHARP
TECH MACHINE 1991

© 12-93
R.S. HIRSCH

1 FT = 0.3048 m   1 FT² = .0929 SQ. M.

COLOR: WHITE – BRIGHT RED LTRS. & METERS.
NO.'S WITH BLACK SHADOW. BLACK
REG. NO.

2.72'
0.5'
0.17
6.0'
4.0'
4.1'
5.55'

.542'
3.88'
4.33'
2.08
4.42'
1.21'
3.15'

5.53'
20.5 FT.
6.25 m
1.63'

19.1 FT
5.82 m
4.5'
0.5'
A B C D E F

1.86'
2.17'

1987-88
"Dillusion"
Jim Harris

This Jensen Cassutt was called "Dillusion" in 1992. It was first called "Gold fever" and painted yellow with white wings. It first showed at Reno in 1987-89. The white paint job existed in 1989. Its qualifying speed in 1987 was 218.757 mph. It was scheduled to show in 1989 but did not qualify. In 1988 it won the Bronze race at 212.554 mph. It was called "Penguin" in 1980.

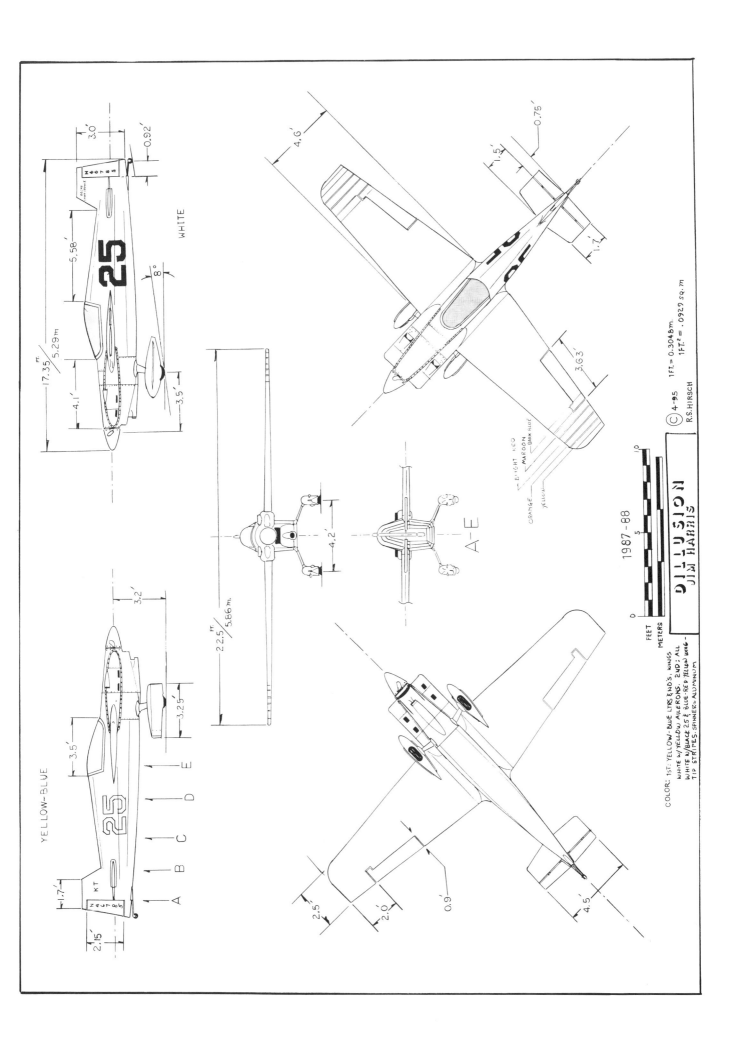

WHITE

YELLOW-BLUE

A B C D E

A-E

COLOR: 1ST: YELLOW-BLUE LTRS ξ NO.'S. WINGS
WHITE W/YELLOW AILERONS. 2ND: ALL
WHITE W/BLACK 25 ξ BLUE-RED /YELLOW WING-
TIP STRIPES. SPINNER= ALUMINUM

BRIGHT RED
MAROON
DARK BLUE
ORANGE
YELLOW

1987-88

DILUSION
JIM HARRIS

© 4-95
R.S. HIRSCH

1 FT.= 0.3048 m.
1 FT.²= .0929 sq. m.

FEET
METERS

1965-70
"Fire Fly"
Ken Burmeister

"Fire Fly" is a Cassutt II built in 1965 by Kenneth H. Burmeister of Kirkland, WA. It was disqualified by the PRPA Technical Committee during the 1966 time trials. It qualified 12th at 159.76 mph at Reno in 1968. It did not show in 1969 but was at Reno for racing in 1970 where it qualified at 177.924 mph. This was the last time it showed up for a race.

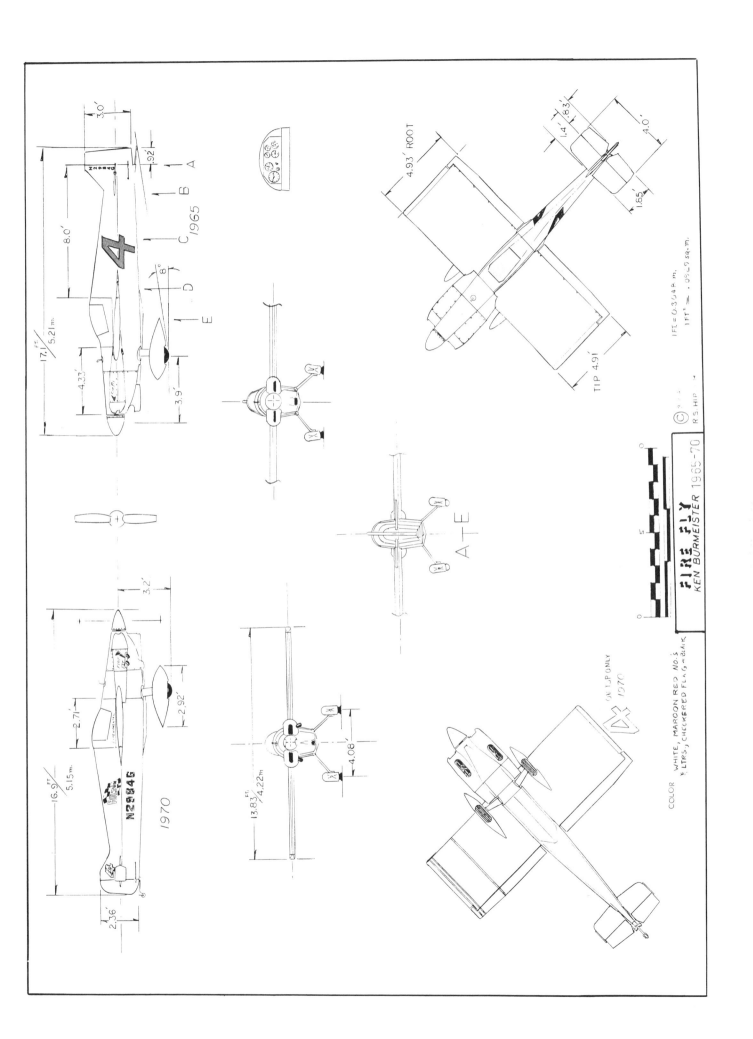

3.0'

.92'

17.1' FT. / 5.21m.

8.0'

4.33'

3.9'

8°

A

B

C 1965

D

E

A—E

A—E 1965

3.2'

2.92'

16.9' FT. / 5.15m.

2.71'

2.36'

N2984G

1970

13.83' FT. / 4.22m

4.08'

ON 1.P ONLY 1970

4.93' ROOT

1.4' — .83'

4.0'

1.65'

TIP 4.91'

1 FT. = 0.3044 m.

1 FT² = .0929 SQ. m.

© 197?
R.S. HIP.

FIREFLY
KEN BURMEISTER 1965-70

COLOR: WHITE, MAROON RED NO.5
& LTRS., CHECKERED FLAG - BLACK

"Lil Quickie"
"Alley Cat"
Ray Cote

This is "Lil Quickie" in 1978 owned by Ray Cote who bought it in 1977. Then a Norton Thomas bought it in 1982 and Dennis West flew it at Reno in 1984. It had several mods and a new paint job with race number 4 up through 1995. It was owned and flown by Ray Cote again in the '90s and called "Alley Cat."

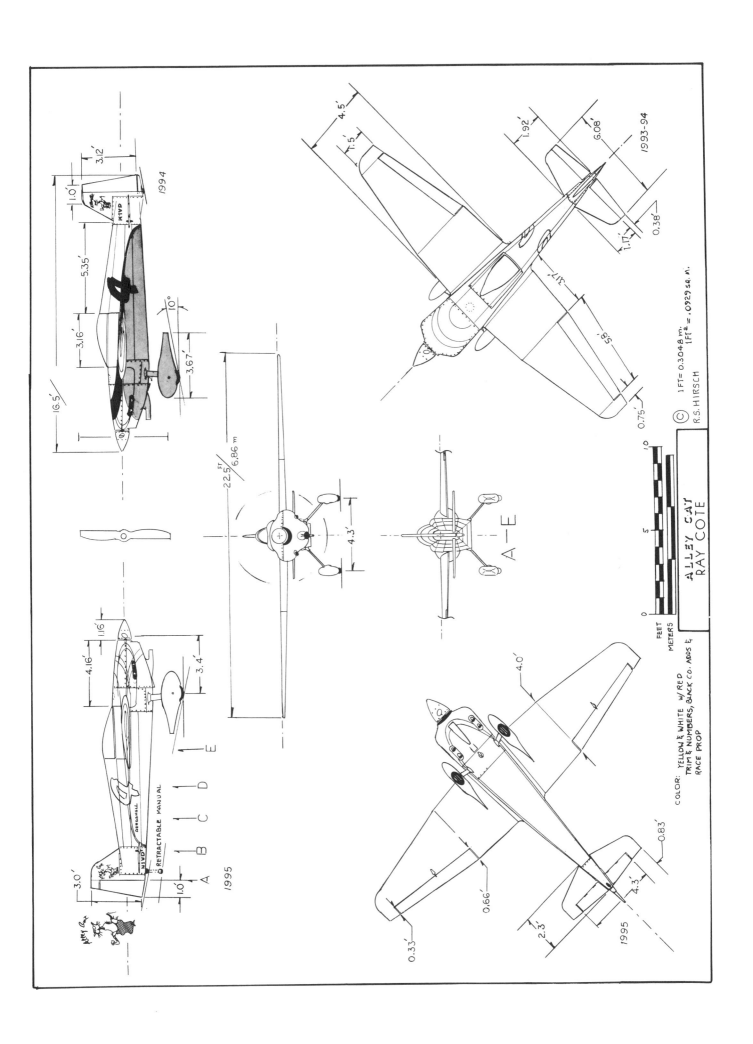

ALLEY CAT
RAY COTE

COLOR: YELLOW & WHITE w/ RED
TRIM & NUMBERS, BLACK CO. ADDS &
RACE PROP

1 FT = 0.3048 m.   1 FT² = .0929 sq. m.

© R.S. HIRSCH

FEET
METERS

"SHOESTRING"
RAY COTE

Ray Cote was quick to see the potential of "Shoestring." He and his crew chief, Clark Huston, showed up at Reno with it and won the Gold Cup each year from 1968 through 1975, and again in 1981. In 1980 he qualified highest but lost out to John Parker. Ray took over Judy Wagner's #44 "Shoestring" and won in 1985. A new wing configuration had been put on it in 1973 designed by an NAA engineer named Ken Stockharger. Ray was backed by Circus-Circus. Ray and his wife wore clown suits.

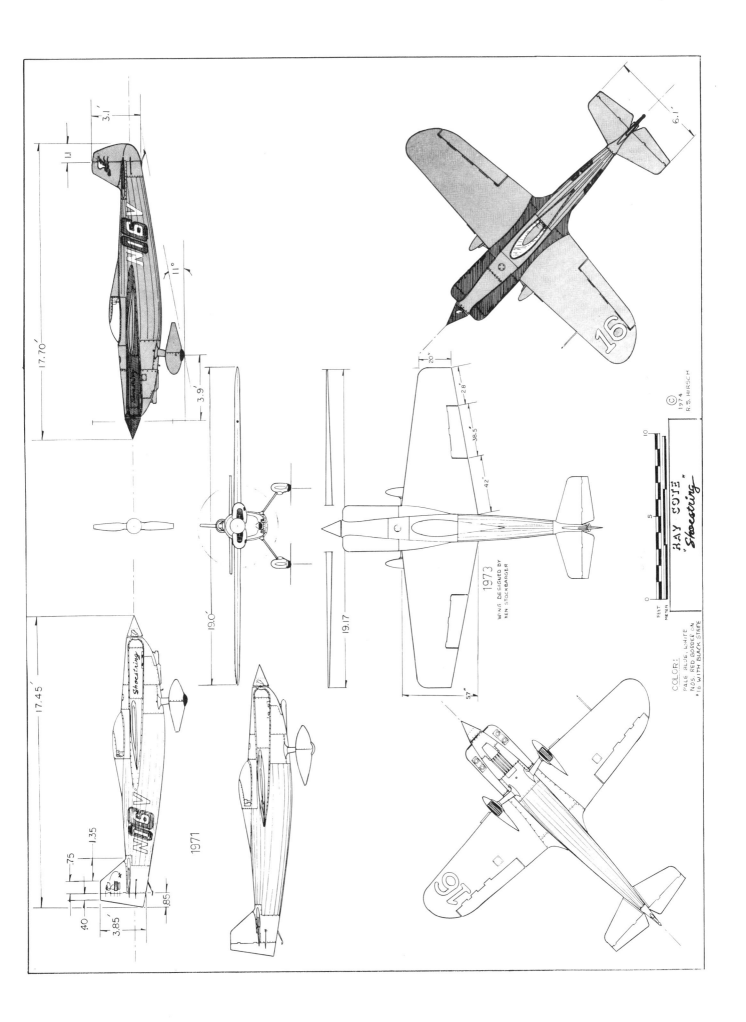

3.1'

1.1

17.70'

N19A

11°

3.9'

6.1'

16

20°

2.8

38.5

42

57"

1973

WING DESIGNED BY
KEN STOCKBARGER

19.17

19.0'

17.45'

Shoestring

N19A

1.35

.75

.40

3.85

.85

1971

16

©
1974
R.S. HIRSCH

RAY COTE
"Shoestring"

COLOR:
PALE BLUE, WHITE
NOS. RED BORDER ON
16 WITH BLACK STRIPE

10

5

0

FEET
METER

Cosmic Wind
"Little Toni"

In 1948 there were three almost identical Cosmic Winds at Cleveland with race numbers 3, 4 and 5. They were flown by Tony Le Vier (3), Herman "Fish" Salmon (4) and Bob Downey (5). Downey also flew #4 at the Fort Wayne Races. "Little Toni" remained unchanged through the years and 22 years later it still reached 201.8 mph flown by a Mr. Roy of Palos Verdes, CA at the Miami Races. Roy bought it in 1968. He metal polished it and flew it as #7 at Reno in 1969 and then in 1971 the plane was painted again like it had been originally. It was sold to Ian McGowen of England and registered G-AAYRS and raced for six more years. #5 was flown to 189 mph by Bob Drew in 1952. It also went to England.

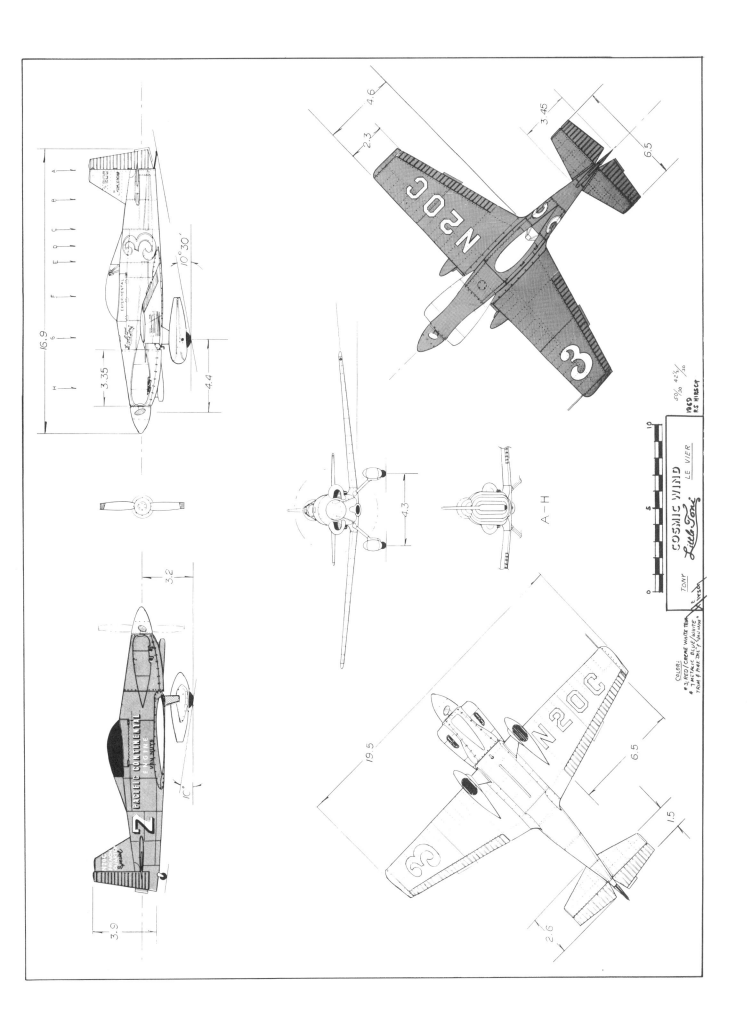

COSMIC WIND
Little Toni

TONY

LE VIER

1969
RS HIRSCH

50/30 42½/30

COLOR:
3 RED/CREME WHITE TRIM
7 METALLIC BLUE/WHITE
TRIM & PALE SKY + YALLAWE

PACIFIC CONTINENTAL
ENGINE
VAN NUYS

A – H

16.9
3.35
4.4
10°30'

3.2
3.9
10°

4.6
2.3
3.45
6.5

4.3

19.5
6.5
1.5
2.6

"MISS COSMIC WIND"
COSMIC WIND

The "Miss Cosmic Wind" was the fourth Cosmic Wind built, a rebuild of #4 "Minnow." It had a new laminar flow wing and registration number. Bill Stead bought it and raced it as #6. John Paul Jones raced it at Fox Field in 1965, and Stead raced it at Reno as "Little Miss Reno." Bob Downey won the first heat at Sparks in 1964 in it. Robert Grieger bought it in 1966. He was the sixth owner. Nick Jones of Augusta, GA flew it at Reno in 1967 and did 169.651 mph. He also did 181.32 mph at Cleveland that year in the semi-finals. In 1969 Roy Berry raced it at Reno but didn't finish. It was again at Reno in 1972 with Damon Berry. It eventually went to the Planes of Fame Air Race Museum in Chino, CA.

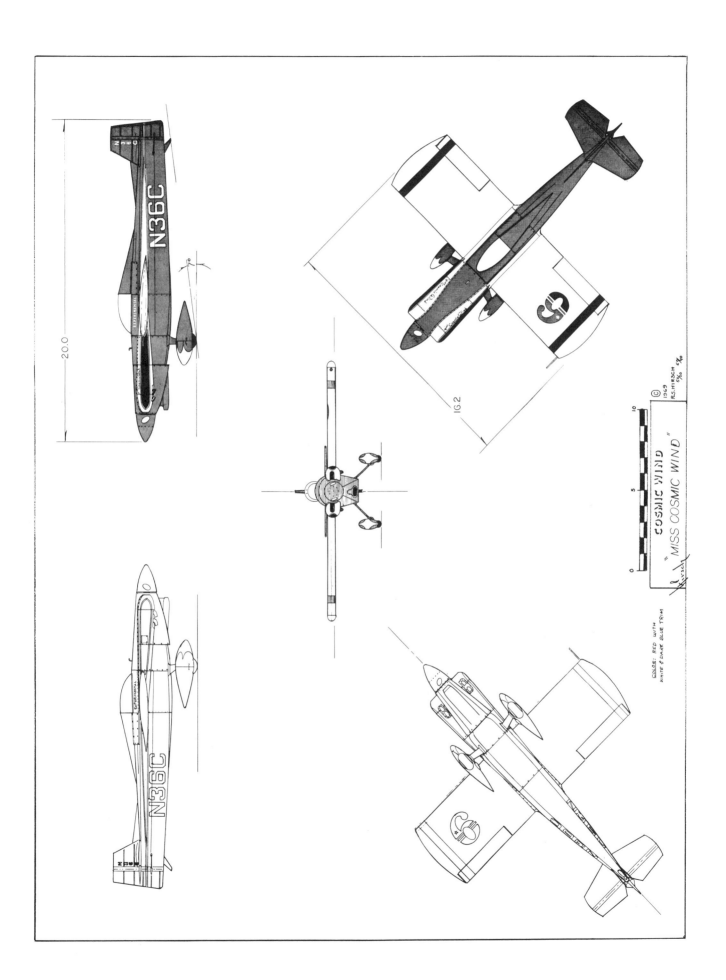

20.0

7°

N36C

N36C

EXPERIMENTAL

3

3

COSMIC WIND
"MISS COSMIC WIND"

COLOR: RED WITH
WHITE & DARK BLUE TRIM

0   5   10

R.S. HIRSCH 6/10
6/10 6/10

© 1969

FIG.2

1992-94
"Okie Stroker"
George Budde

The N 102 registration number was taken from a CAA DC-3 closed out at the Oklahoma City Center for this Cassutt named "Okie Stroker." It is owned by George Budde of Midwest City, OK. It has existed since 1992 and qualified at Reno 14th at 215.889 mph in 1993 and 207.142 mph in 1994. It was also raced at Paso Robles, CA by Bobby Budde. George Budde also flew Cassutt number 19 at Reno.

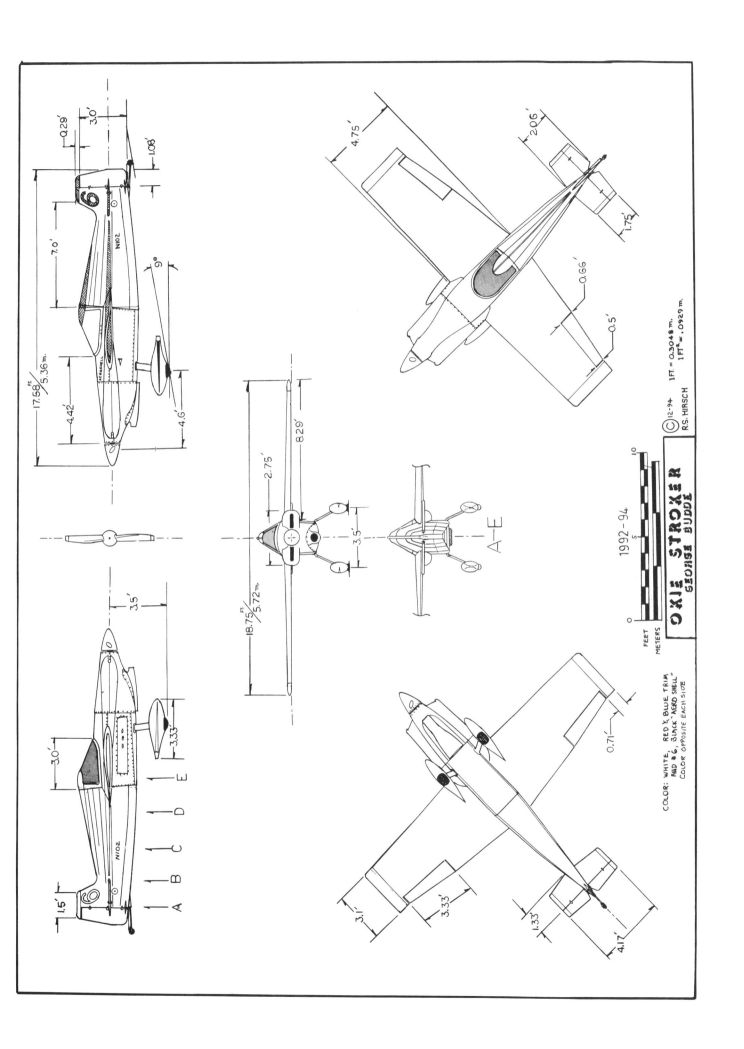

OXIE STROKER

GEORGE BUDDE

1992-94

FEET
METERS

COLOR: WHITE, RED & BLUE TRIM
AND #6, BLACK "AERO SHELL"
COLOR OPPOSITE EACH SIDE

© 12-94   1FT.= 0.3048 m.
R.S. HIRSCH   1FT.= .0929 m.

A-E

1964-73
"SLOW MOTION"
TERRILL

The Terrill "Slow Motion" was designed and built by Howard and Dale Terrill in 1963 and raced at Reno in 1964. It qualified 23rd down out of a group of 24. It was owned by Don DeWalt of Los Angeles. In 1973 it did not get off in the Medallion Race which was its only entry to the various heat races. It underwent mods on the prop, spinner, wheels, canopy and engine cowl in 1972 and was painted maroon and silver. In its early configuration it was red and white with a black number 5.

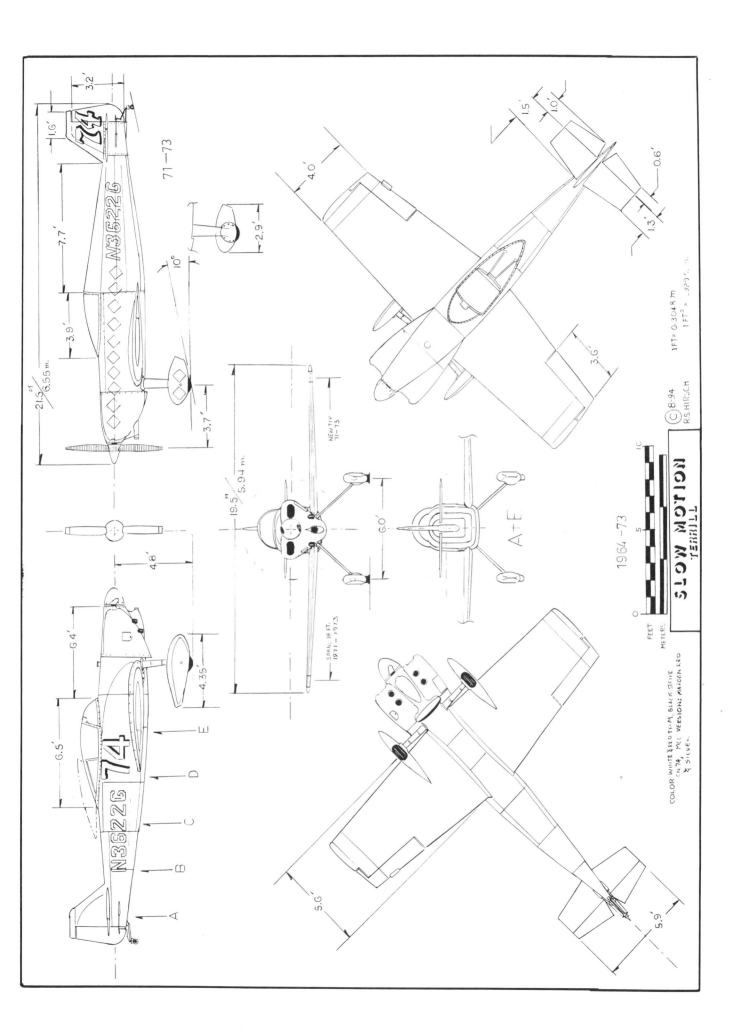

71-73

N3622G

21.5'ᶠᵗ / 6.55 m.

10°

2.9'

3.2'

1.6'

7.7'

3.9'

3.7'

4.8'

19.5'ᶠᵗ / 5.94 m.

NEW TIV
71-73

SPAN: 19 FT.
1971 - 1973

6.4'

6.5'

4.35'

A   B   C   D   E

1.5'

1.0'

0.6'

1.3'

4.0'

3.6'

5.6'

5.9'

6.0'

A+E

1964 - 73

COLOR: WHITE & RED TRIM, BLACK STRIPE
ON 74. MCL VERSION: MAROON RED
& SILVER

SLOW MOTION
TERRILL

1FT= 0.3048 m
1FT² = .093 sq.m.

© 8-94
R.S. HIRSCH

0   5   10
FEET
METERS

1966-74
"SHOSHNICK"
HOWARD TERRILL

"Shoshnick" was built in 1966 by Howard Terrill. It qualified 8th highest at Cleveland in 1968 and 4th at Reno in 1969. It was forced out of a race at Cleveland when a seagull smashed the canopy (to say nothing of the condition of the seagull). It came to Reno in 1969 with Salvadore Lanese as pilot and placed 2nd in the Consolation race. A new canopy design and increasing the tail surfaces in 1970 corrected the porpoising. In 1970 Lanese also placed 2nd in the Consolation race at Ft. Lauderdale, FL. It was active up through 1974. It was renamed "Deja Vu" which is French for "having seen something before."

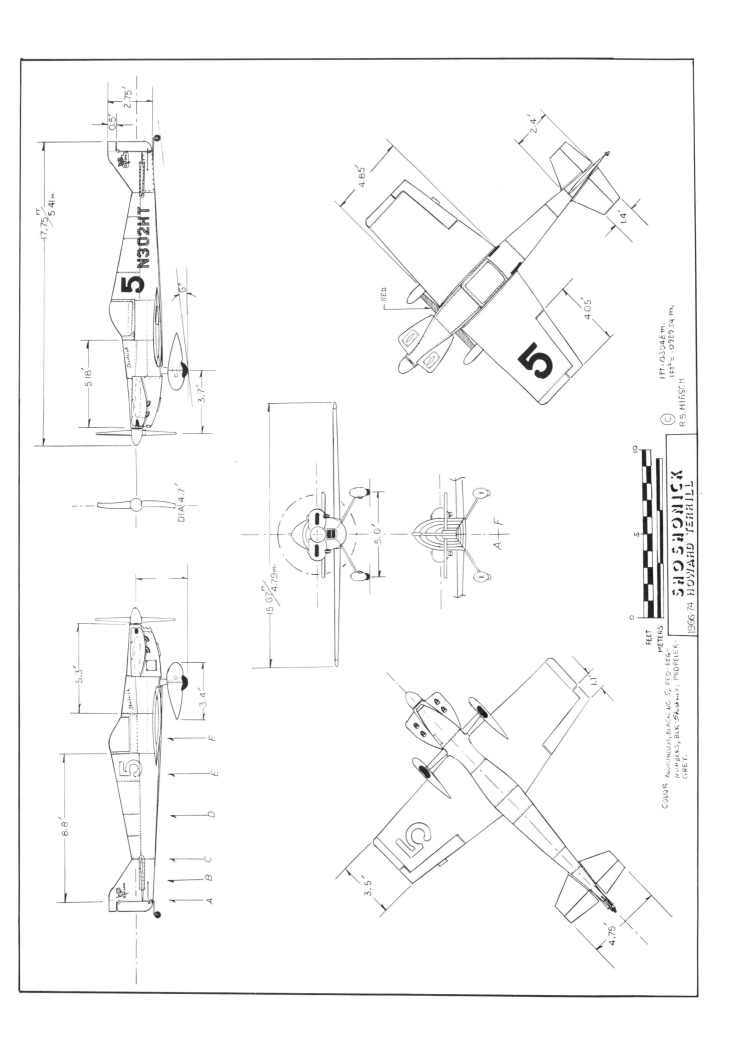

17.75 FT / 5.41m.

2.75'

0.5'

N302HT

5

6°

5.18'

3.7'

DIA 4.7'

5.3'

3.4'

8.8'

5

A B C D E F

4.85

2.4'

1.4'

RED

4.05'

5

1 FT = .3048 m.
1 FT² = .0929 SQ m.

© R.S. HIRSCH

15.67 FT / 4.79m.

5.0'

A — F

3.5'

4.75'

1.1'

5

FEET
METERS

0 5 10

SHOSHONICK

1966-74 HOWARD TERRILL

COLOR: ALUMINUM, BLACK NO. 5, RED REG-
NUMBERS, BLK Shoshonick, PROPELER-
GREY.

1959-79
"POOPSIE DOLL"
HOWARD TERRILL

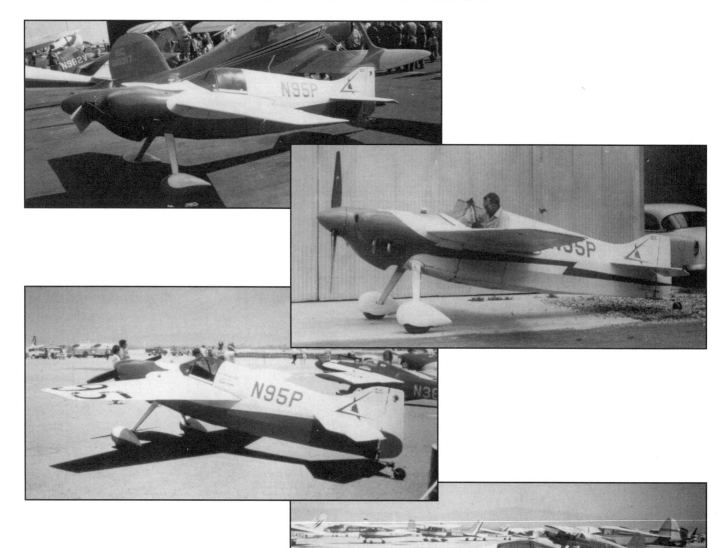

Construction on the HLT-100 "Poopsie Doll" N-121W was started in 1957 and its first flight was in June 1960. James H. Wilson of Dallas, TX used race number 21 when it was called "Baby Cyclone." He raced it a couple of times before selling it to build #34 "Snoopy." Howard Terrill rebuilt it in eight months in his spare time and re-registered it N-95P and used race number 95. It flew as modified in September 1970. It had a Cessna spring gear.

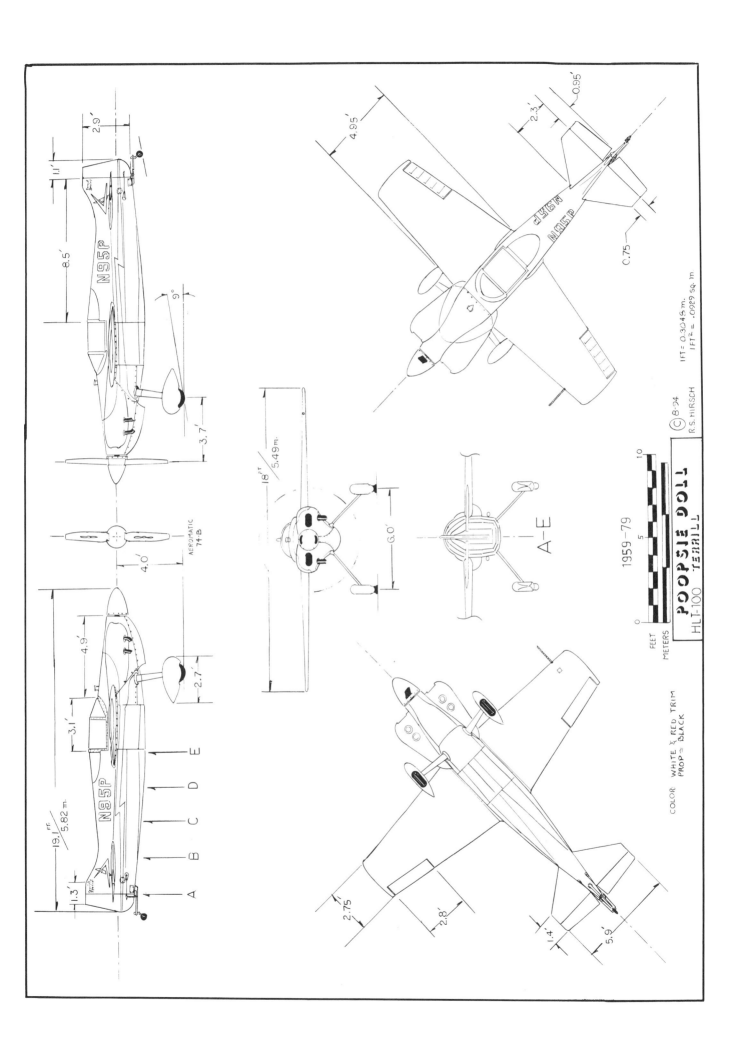

2.9'

1.1'

N95P

8.5'

9°

3.7'

AEROMATIC 74-B

4.0'

4.9'

3.1'

2.7'

N95P

19.1 FT / 5.82 m.

1.3'

A B C D E

18 FT / 5.49 m.

6.0'

A-E

4.95

2.3'

0.95'

N95P

N95P

0.75

2.75

2.8'

1.4'

5.9'

COLOR WHITE & RED TRIM
PROP ≈ BLACK

1959-79

POOPSIE DOLL

HL1-100 TERRILL

1 FT = 0.3045 m.
1 FT² = .0929 SQ. m.

© 8-94
R.S. HIRSCH

10

5

0

FEET
METERS

CASSUTT
"GREY GHOST"
MODEL E

This Garland-Pack model E was built in 1959 at Nashville, TN and was named "Grey Ghost." It was first flown on September 10, 1959 and qualified at its first meet at 192.3 mph. It also was known as "Little Bit" and "Little A-Go-Go." It was raced at Fort Wayne in September 1959 by Paul Booth. In 1965 at Lancaster, Bud Jurg raced it, and then sold it to Herbert Jack Jella who rebuilt it for the 1968 Reno races where he did only 187.044 mph. In 1969 he was sixth in the finals at 201.399. It was absent from Reno from 1970 through 1981, but showed up a couple of times after 1981.

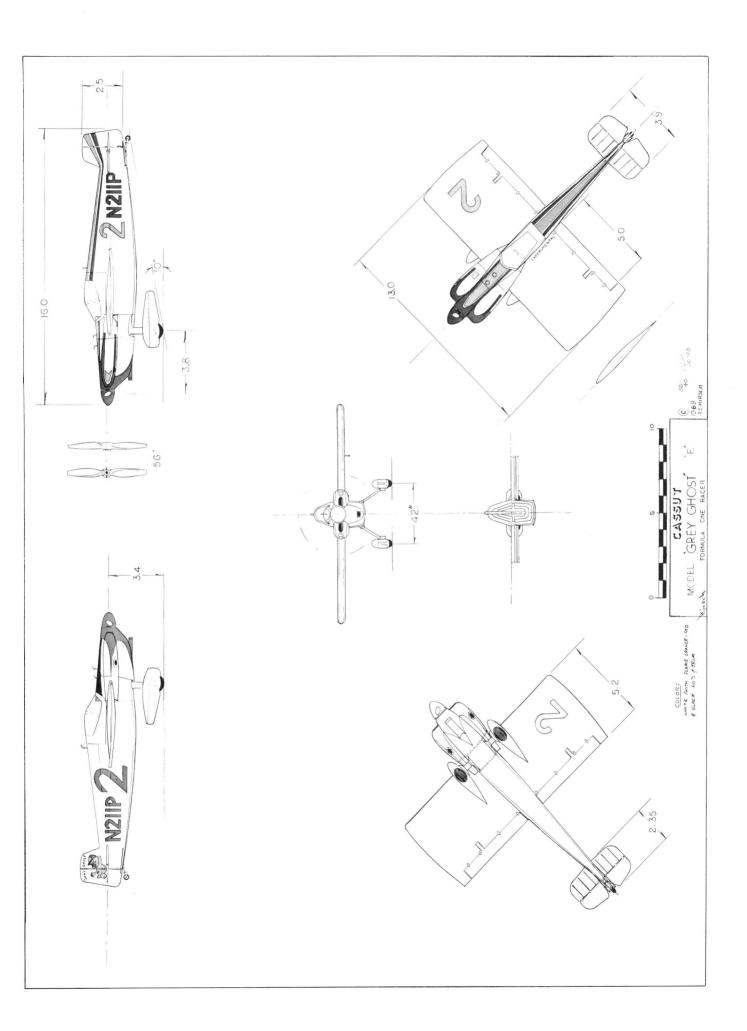

2.5

16.0

N21IP 2

10°

3.8

5G"

42"

3.9

13.0

5.0

EXPERIMENTAL

10

5

0

COLOR:
WHITE WITH FLAME ORANGE-RED
& BLACK NO'S & TRIM

CASSUT
MODEL "GREY GHOST" 'E'
FORMULA ONE RACER

© 1969 R.S.HIRSCH

N21IP 2

GREY GHOST

3.4

5.2

2.35

1977
"POLE CAT"
PR-2

 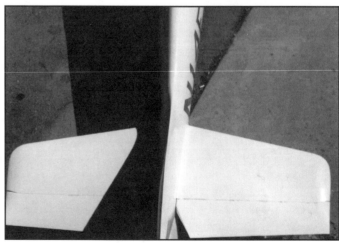

The modified Cassutt "Pole Cat" appeared in 1976-78, owned by Ernie Prosch and called PR-2. It showed at Reno in 1977 where Bob Reinseth placed 5th in the Gold race at 216.65 mph. In the earlier Consolation race it also placed 5th at 224.688 mph. It was purchased by the Japan Air Racing Team in May 1978, and was destroyed at Mojave, CA on June 14, 1978, killing the pilot, Tateo Fukatsu.

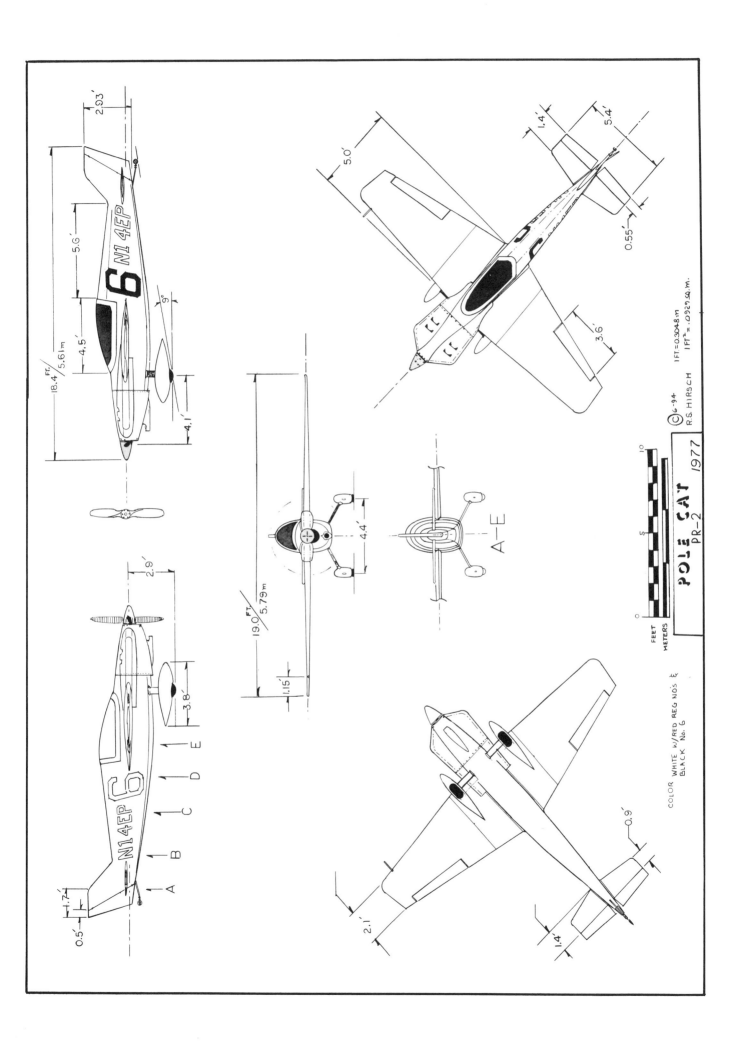

2.93'

18.4 FT./5.61m

5.6'

4.5'

9°

4.1'

N14EP 9

5.0'

1.4'

5.4'

0.55'

3.6'

2.9'

3.8'

N14EP 9

A   B   C   D   E

0.5'

1.7'

19.0 FT./5.79m

4.4'

1.15'

A—E

0.9'

2.1'

1.4'

COLOR WHITE W/RED REG NOS &
BLACK No. 6

© 6-94
R.S. HIRSCH

1FT=0.3048m
1FT²=.0929 sq.m.

POLE CAT
PR-2   1977

FEET
METERS

0   5   10

1971-72
"Cheeta"
Cassutt M III

    "Cheeta" was the eleventh Cassutt, of about 130, built and was completed in 1966 by Herschel Lemoron, and raced by Don Davis in 1970 at Wilson, NC. It had been sold to William L. Sullivan, a Kentucky State Senator from Henderson, in 1968. He raced it at Reno and Miami, placing 4th in the Silver at Reno in 1972. It had the new Jim Wilson wing and fuselage mods in 1973.

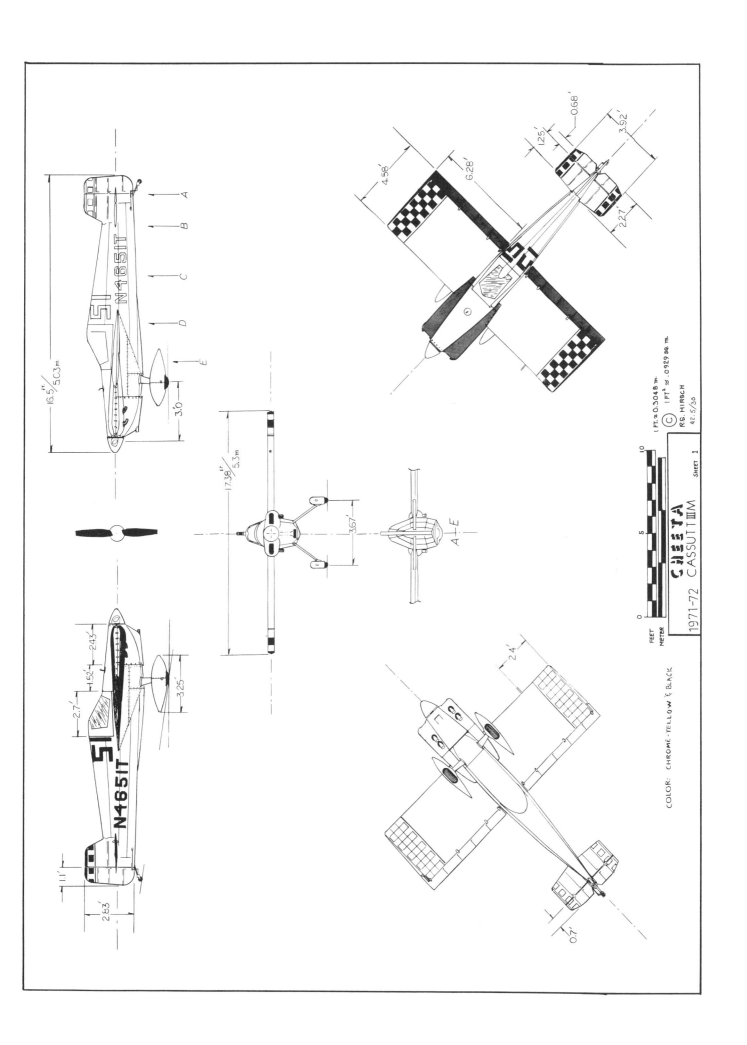

COLOR: CHROME-YELLOW & BLACK

1 FT. ≈ 0.3048 m. 1 FT² ≈ .0929 sq. m.

© R.G. HIRSCH
42.5/30

FEET
METER

CHEETA
1971-72 CASSUTT IIIM   SHEET 1

1972-74
"ANACONDA-1"
FROM "CHEETA"

In 1973 Senator Sullivan rebuilt the Cassutt "Cheeta" (M III) and renamed it "Anaconda." The yellow and black paint job was changed to green and chrome yellow. The new name was for one of the lawyer's clients. It was raced at Reno in 1972-3 and in '72 did 197.44 mph and was 4th in the Silver race. In 1974 it crashed at Evansville in a forced landing from a qualification run and was damaged extensively.

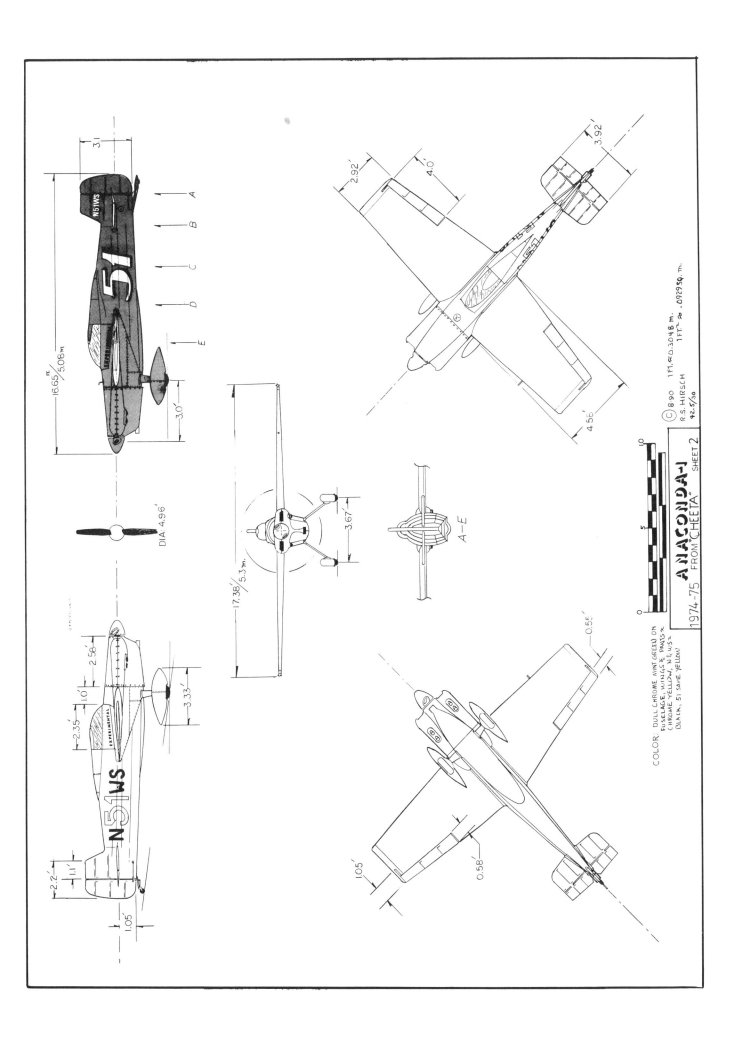

DIA: 4.96'

A — E

17.38'/5.3 m.

3.67'

COLOR: DULL CHROME MINT GREEN ON
FUSELAGE, WINGS & PANTS &
CHROME YELLOW, N & W S &
BLACK, 51 SAME YELLOW

© 8·90   1 FT. ≈ 0.3048 m.   1 FT.² ≈ .0929 SQ. m.
R.S. HIRSCH
42.5/30

ANACONDA I
1974-75   FROM "CHEETA"   SHEET 2

1986-89
"ANACONDA-2"
"ANACONDA-1" MODIFED

The newer "Anaconda-2" is a rebuild of the earlier one. It had some mods in the elevator area, the cockpit, and airframe aft of the cockpit. The new colors were orange and white, and it raced at Reno in 1975. It was shipped to France in this configuration but with a green wing, it was detained for awhile by the government in 1976. It eventually qualified in France at 220.5 mph at Le Castellet. It was raced in England as G-BUGM and in France as F.PYNM and N-51WS back at Sturgis, KY in 1977. It won the Reno Silver race in 1975 at 215.892 mph.

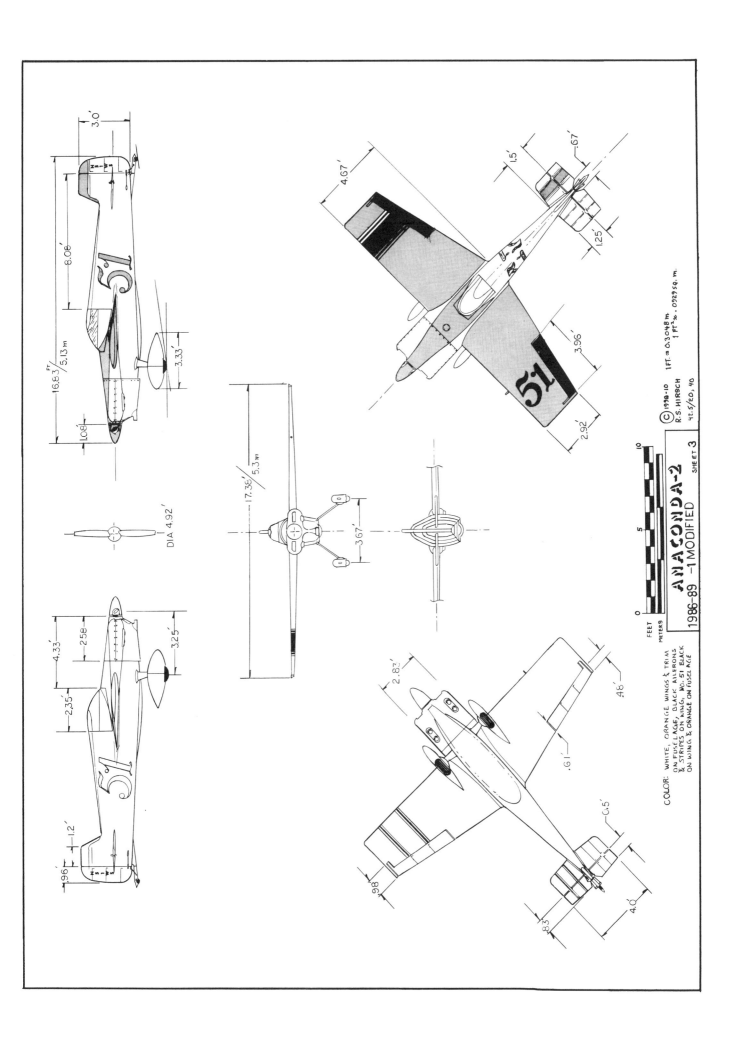

DIA 4.92'

COLOR: WHITE, ORANGE WINGS & TRIM
ON FUSELAGE, BLACK AILERONS
& STRIPES ON WING, NO. 51 BLACK
ON WING & ORANGE ON FUSELAGE

© 1998-10   1 FT. ≈ 0.3048 m.
R.S. HIRSCH   1 FT.² ≈ .0929 SQ. m.
42.5/20, 40

ANACONDA-2
1986-89 -1 MODIFIED   SHEET 3

FEET
METERS

"MOTHER HOLIDAY"
NICK JONES

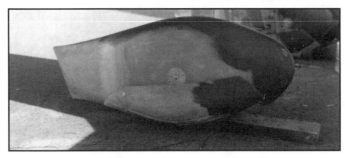

The Cassutt here has been modified and its unpainted natural wood varnished wing panels made it stand out. It was built in 1970-71 and raced at Wilson, NC on May 15-16th in 1971. It was built and flown by Howell "Nick" Jones of Augusta, GA and placed 3rd in the finals at 216.6 mph. It had two names: "Ol Mable" and "Mother Holiday" (which prevails). It raced at Cape May, NJ, at Cleveland and at Reno. At Miami it was flown by Jack Lowers. At Reno, Nick made a set of clam-shell door covers for the exposed parts of the wheels. In 1972 he extended the ailerons to the wingtips for better lateral control.

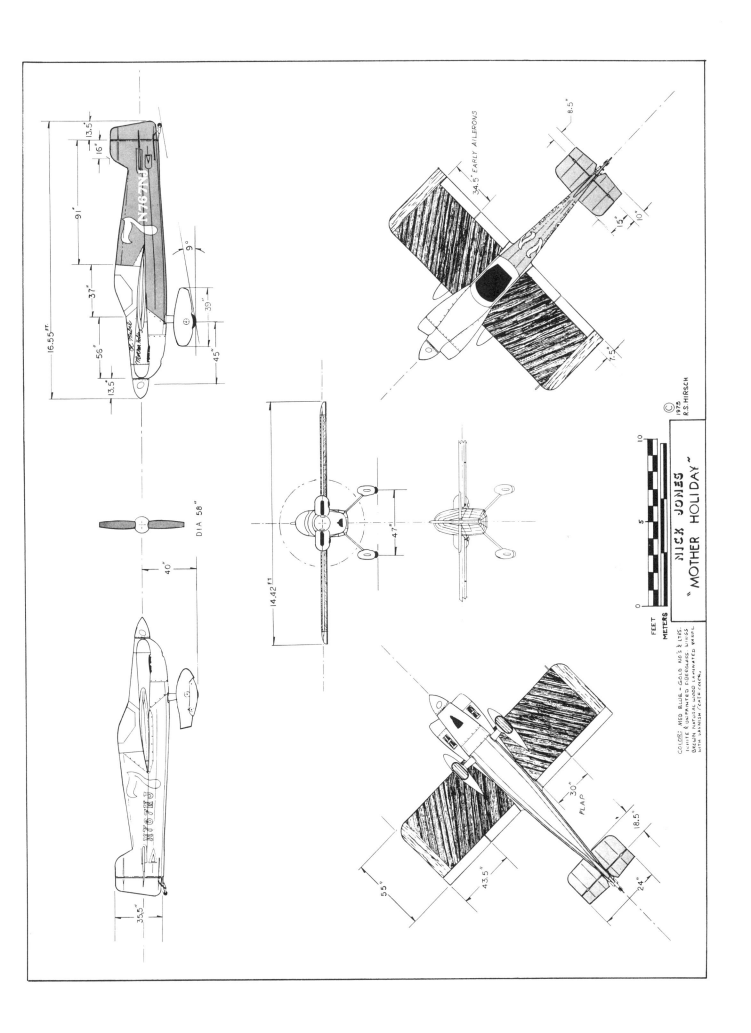

13.5"
16"
91"
37"
56"
13.5"
16.55 FT.
N767NU
J. Mill
Morton Holiday

9°
39"
45"

DIA 58"
40"

34.5° EARLY AILERONS
8.5"
15"
10"
7.5"

14.42 FT
4 7"

NICK JONES
"MOTHER HOLIDAY"

© 1975
R.S.HIRSCH

0   5   10
FEET
METERS

COLORS: MED. BLUE - GOLD NO'S & LTRS.
(WHITE & UNPAINTED FIBERGLASS) WINGS
BROWN NATURAL WOOD LAMINATED MANFL.
WITH VARNISH (COAT/COLOR)

30"
FLAP
18.5"
55"
43.5"
24"

N767NU
35.5"

1975-78
"Proud Bird"
SL-1

 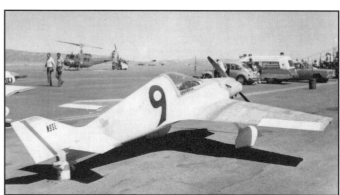

The SL-1 "Proud Bird" was built and flown by Fred Wofford. It showed up at Mojave in 1976. It was 3rd fastest with a qualifying time of 237.444 mph and won the 1-B and Gold races. At Reno it reached the highest qualifying time at 237.362 mph but did not get into the finals. It was listed as Schultz-Le Mire SL-1. In 1977 it qualified 3rd at 225.841 mph and placed 3rd in the Gold race at 223.217 mph at Reno. Fred Wofford's first plane was a Cassutt called "Gold Dust," and later called "Cyclone."

see Rivets... planform

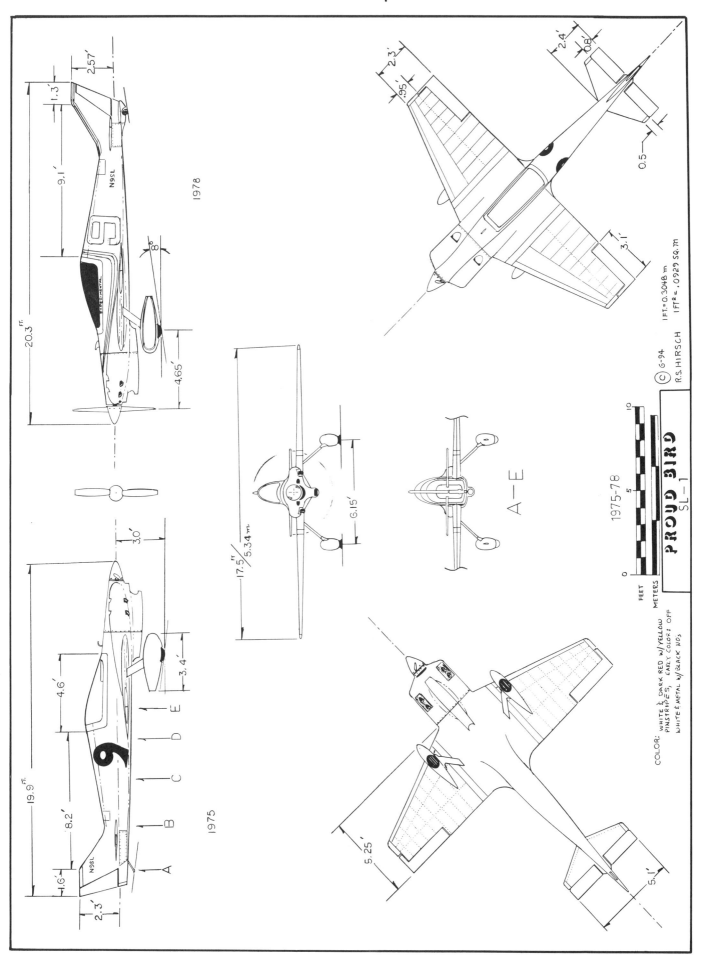

1978

1975

A—E

1975-78

PROUD BIRD
SL—1

1 FT = 0.3048 m
1 FT² = .0929 SQ.M

© 6-94
R.S. HIRSCH

COLOR: WHITE & DARK RED W/ YELLOW
PINSTRIPES, EARLY COLOR & OFF
WHITE & METAL W/ BLACK Nos

"FANG"
GEORGE OWL
MODEL OR-70-1

This Owl OR-70-1 "Fang" was raced at Point Mugu, CA in 1972 and was built in 1970 by Bill Warwick and showed up at Reno with no paint job in 1971. It qualified at 203.77 mph. It was designed by George Owl. Jim Stevenson of North Hollywood, CA qualified it at Reno in 1973 at 207.294 mph.

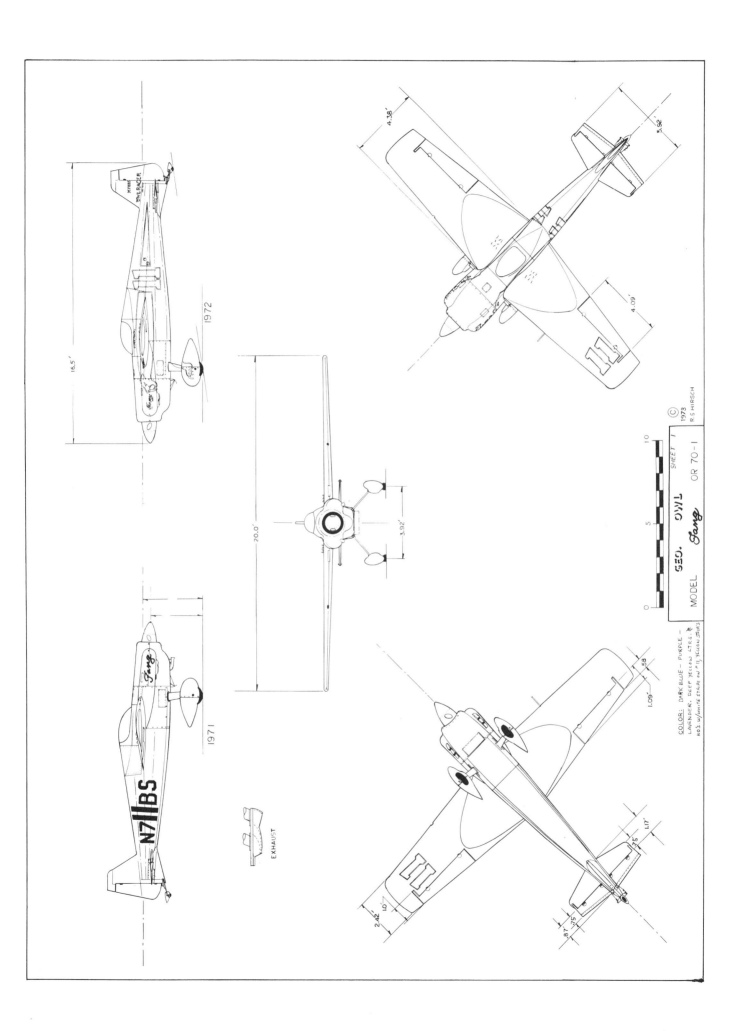

COLOR: DARK BLUE — PURPLE —
LAVENDER: DEEP YELLOW LTRS. &
NOS W/WHITE STRIPE ON #11, YELLOW STRIPE

GEO. OWL
MODEL Sang   OR 70–1

SHEET 1
© 1973
R.S.HIRSCH

1972

16.5'

20.0'

3.92'

1971

EXHAUST

4.38'

5.92'

4.09'

.58
1.09'

1.17'
.75

2.42'
.07'

.87'
.75

"POGO"
GEORGE OWL
MODEL OR-65-2

The OR-65-2 was designed by George Owl and built by John Alford in the summer/fall of 1969. In 1969 it placed 5th in the St. Louis Consolation race and again 5th in the Reno finals at 208.90 mph. It was the first all new F-1 at Reno since 1966. Joan and John Alford brought it to Reno around 1971 where it was raced by Joan who had been a pilot for 26 years. She was a 44-year old mother of six and grandmother of four. She was the beauty queen of the pylons. In 1972 the plane was sold to Donald Beck who raced it to 7th place in the finals at Reno. He also raced it at the Miami races in 1973, and in 1973 sold it to Logan J. Hines of Conoga Park, CA.

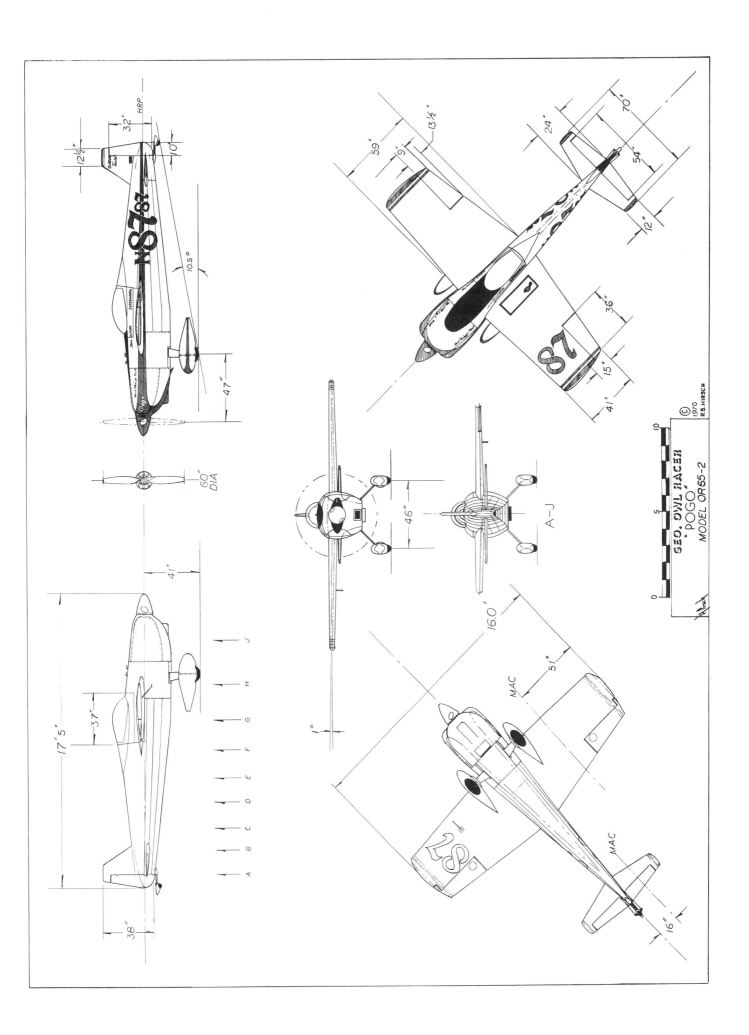

GEO. OWL RACER
"POGO"
MODEL OR65-2

© 1970 R.S. HIRSCH

1988-89
"PUSHY CAT"
JIM MILLER

James Miller built this JM-2 type "Pushy Cat" in 1987 after selling his "Texas Gem" in 1986 to Errol Robertson. This ship was stripped of a lot of extras. Miller sat on the fuselage bottom. It was built of graphite which is lighter and stronger than fiberglass, saving about 65 pounds. It was built to accommodate Miller's own body of 145 pounds. The plane accelerates quickly and usually stays out in front at least for a good part of the eight laps.

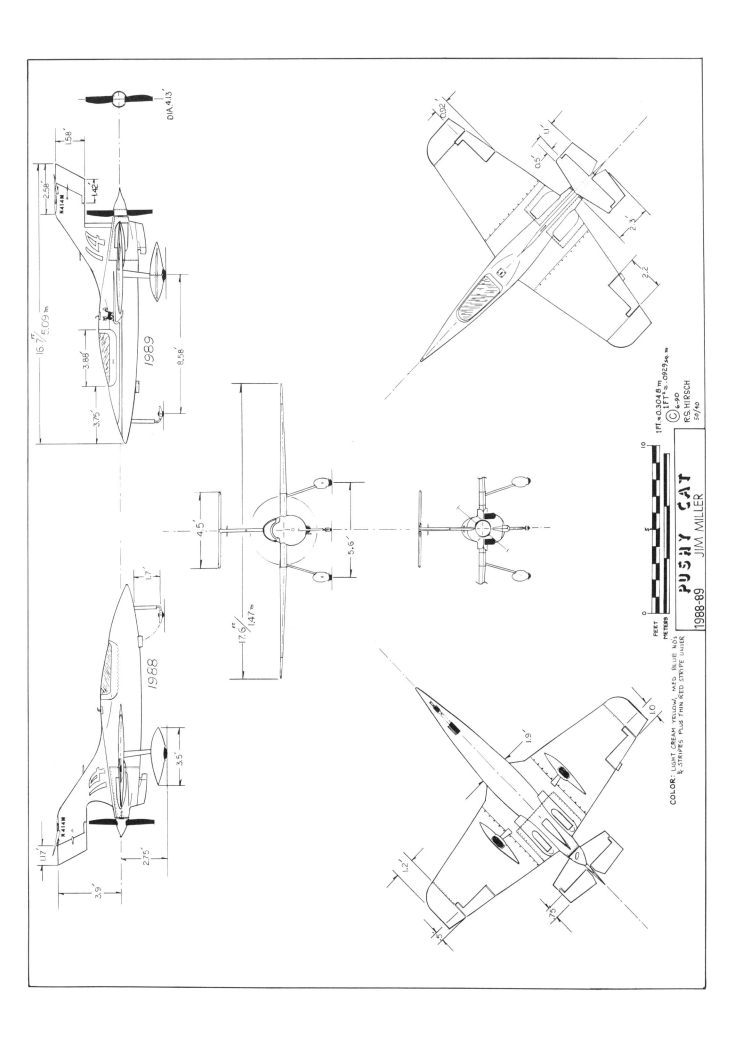

DIA. 4.13'

1.58'

2.58

N414M

1.42'

14

1989

16.7' FT / 5.09 m

3.88'

8.58

3.75

0.92

0.5'

1.1'

2.3

2.2

1.9'

1.0

1.2'

.75

.5

1.17'

1.7

1988

3.5'

N414M

3.9'

2.75

4.5'

5.6'

17.6' FT / 1.47 m

1 FT. = 0.3048 m
1 FT² = .0929 sq. m

© 6-90
R.S. HIRSCH
50/40

FEET
METERS
10
5
0

PUSHY CAT
1988-89   JIM MILLER

COLOR: LIGHT CREAM YELLOW, MED BLUE NO'S
& STRIPES PLUS THIN RED STRIPE UNDER

1964-74
"OLE TIGER"
BOB DOWNEY

In 1965 "Little Gem" became "Ole Tiger" and at Reno placed 3rd in the finals at 194.44 mph. In 1968 Bob Downey, the pilot, turned in 217.99 at Maryland but cut a pylon. At Cleveland in 1968 "Ole Tiger" was second behind "Rivets" in the finals but won race 2-A. At Reno in 1968, Downey again was behind Falck only a few yards in heat 1-B, both above 213 mph, but Downey won heat 2-A. Frank Johnson was crew chief. After some air intake design changes to affect engine cooling, the plane was doing 223.14 mph by 1972.

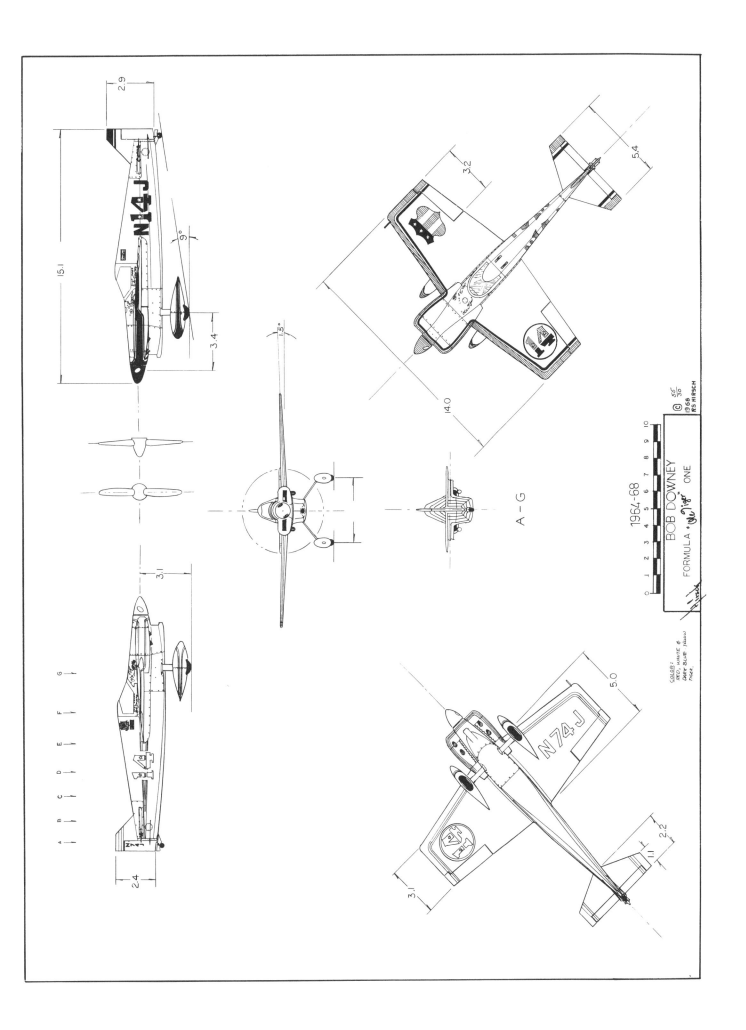

N14J

2.9

15.1

9°

3.4

1.5°

3.1

A B C D E F G

2.4

A – G

3.2

5.4

14.0

N74J

5.0

3.1

2.2

1.1

1964–68

BOB DOWNEY

FORMULA *Liber* ONE

COLOR:
RED, WHITE &
DARK BLUE (TRIM)
TIGER.

© 55/30
1968
R'S HIRSCH

0 1 2 3 4 5 6 7 8 9 10

1974-81
"OLE TIGER"
BOB DOWNEY

New wingtips and a taller tail were tried in 1974-5 but the qualifying time at Reno was a slow 208.897 mph. The speed times stayed this way when Roy Berry bought it and flew it at Mojave in 1978. Bob Downey crashed it and was killed at Reno in 1981 during time trials.

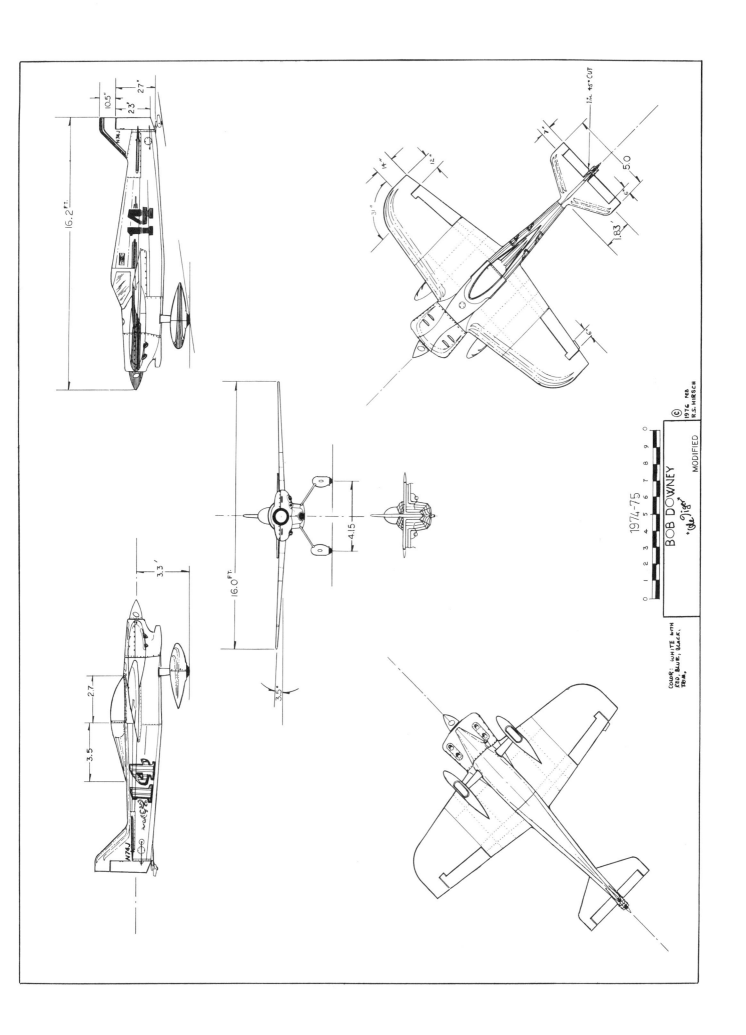

1974-75

BOB DOWNEY
"Skier"

MODIFIED

© 1976 FEB
R.S. HIRSCH

COLOR: WHITE WITH
RED, BLUE, BLACK,
TRIM.

16.2 FT.

10.5" 23° 27°

16.0 FT.

4.15

3.5°

3.3' 2.7' 3.5'

14" 12" 31"

5.0

1.83'

6' 6"

1 IN. 45° CUT

1973
"Loki"
Ernest Prosch

Ernest Prosch of Las Vegas designed and built "Loki" for the 1973 races. Robert Reinseth was the pilot at Reno and Prosch at the Miramar races. The engine was from Reinseth's #72 Cassutt. It did 198.529 mph during the qualifying test at Reno but placed last in the Consolation race at 193.852 mph. In 1976 Robert Drew qualified and tested this racer (now named "Snapshot") at 186.207 mph at Reno. Marc DeLay of Anaheim, CA purchased it from Prosch and raced it at Reno in 1976.

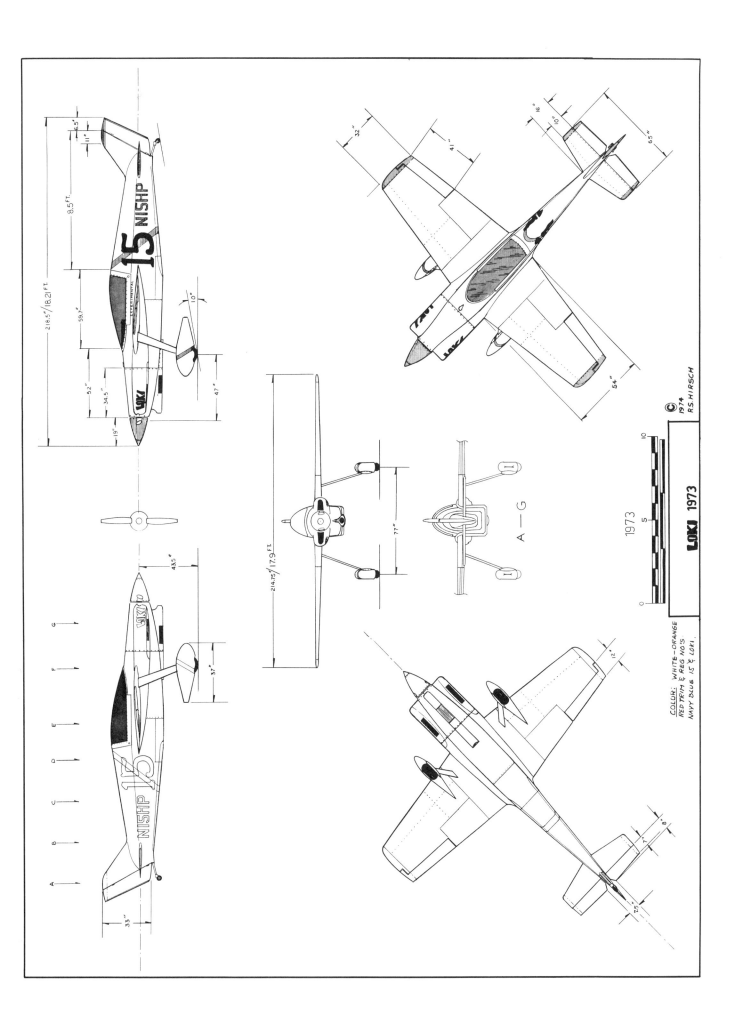

6.5"
11"
8.5 FT.
218.5"/18.21 FT.
59.7"
15 NISHP
EXPERIMENTAL
LOKI
52"
34.5
19"
47"
10°

43.5"
NISHP 15
LOKI
57"

33"

A B C D E F G

32"
41"
16"
10"
6.5"
54"

214.75"/17.9 FT.
77"

A — G

1973

12"
7"
8"
7.5"

COLOR: WHITE—ORANGE
RED TRIM & REG NO'S.
NAVY BLUE 15 & LOKI.

© 1974
R.S. HIRSCH

LOKI 1973

0 5 10

"Aquarius"
Marion Baker

Marion Baker's "Aquarius" had been modified into sort of a bubble canopy version of his No. 80 all-metal home design. Wingtip, engine exhaust and cowl changes, along with a larger rudder made this version different in shape from No. 80. Baker was well-known by his often-winning Cassutt "Boo Ray" No. 81.

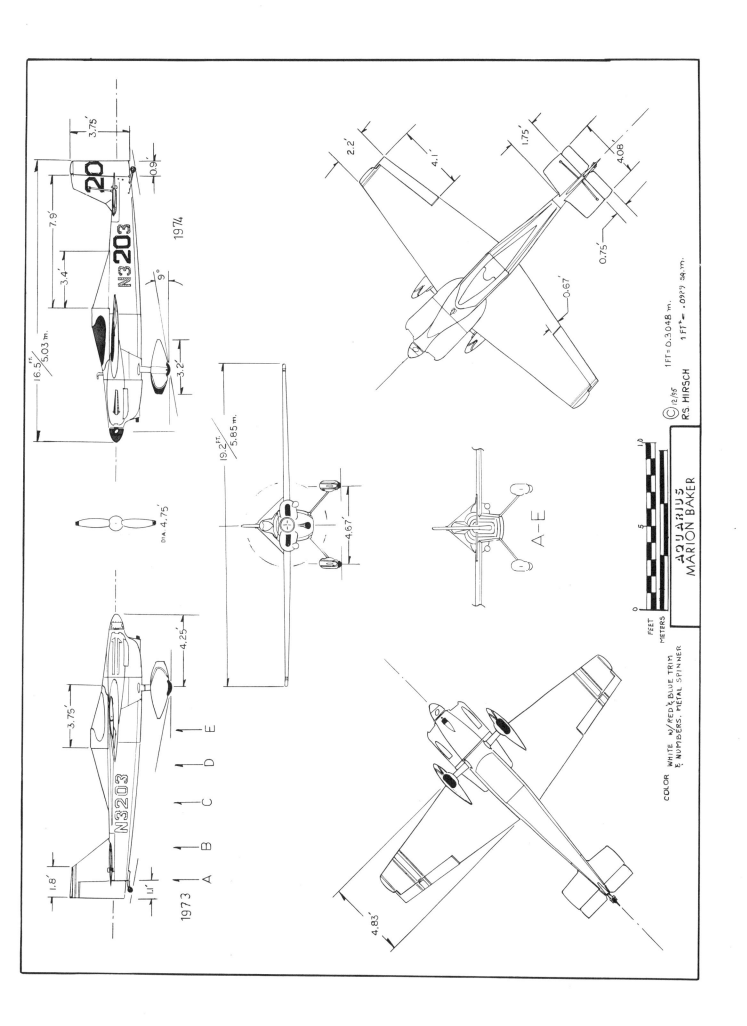

3.75

0.9'

7.9'

3.4'

9°

16.5' FT. / 5.03 m.

3.2'

1974

2.2'

4.1'

1.75'

4.08

0.75'

0.67'

DIA. 4.75'

19.2 FT. / 5.85 m.

4.67'

A-E

4.25'

3.75'

1.8'

1.1'

1973   A   B   C   D   E

4.83'

COLOR WHITE w/ RED & BLUE TRIM
& NUMBERS. METAL SPINNER

© 12/95
R.S. HIRSCH

1 FT = 0.3048 m.   1 FT² = .0929 SQ. m.

AQUARIUS
MARION BAKER

FEET
METERS

0   5   1.0

1948-67 Steve Wittman
"Bonzo II"
Continental C-85

Steve J. Wittman's "Bonzo" was built in 1948. This wire-braced wood wing racer is one of the midget racers most famous aircraft. Steve paid attention to small details such as one tail wheel for cross country and a smaller one for racing. He developed the much copied spring landing gear struts in the 30s. Steve, who was 90 in 1995, made his last acrobatic flight in "Bonzo" at Oshkosh, WI before giving it to the Museum. He and his second wife, Paula, were killed on April 27, 1995, when his "Buttercup" (his private plane) broke up in flight. Steve Wittman made his mark and stands as one of the real giants in air racing and private aviation with his engineering and piloting skills.

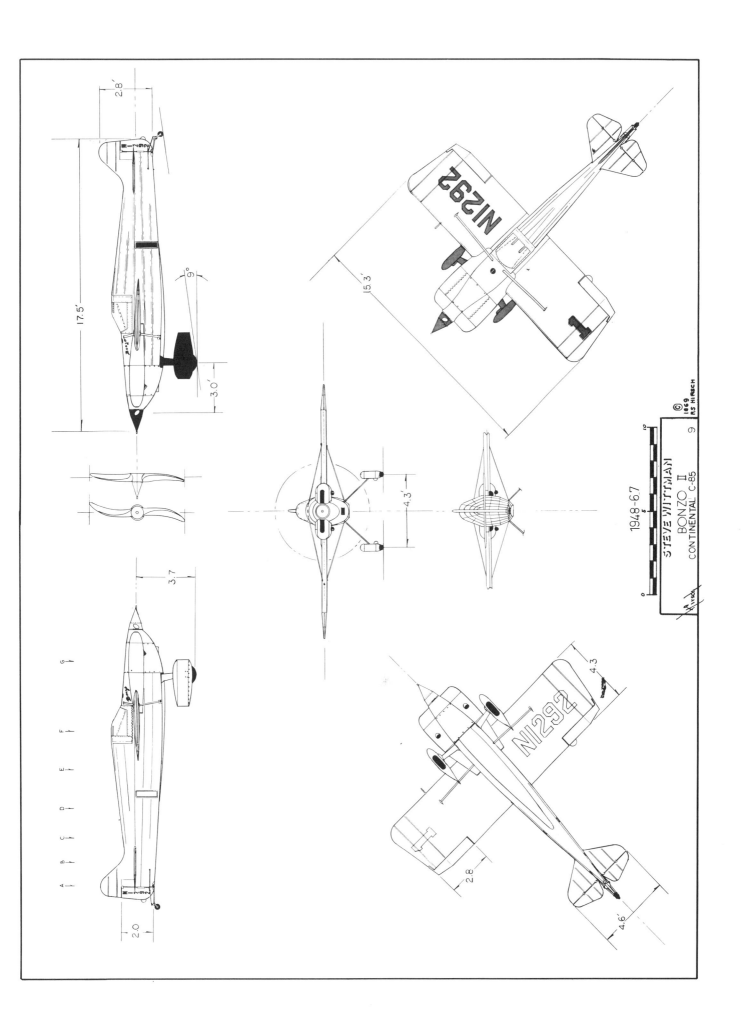

2.8'

17.5'

9°

3.0'

15.3'

3.7

4.3'

2.0

N1292

N1292

N1292

4.3

2.8

4.6'

STEVE WITTMAN

BONZO II

CONTINENTAL C-85

1948-67

9

© 1969 RS HIRSCH

A B C D E F G

1970-74
"SPOOKY"
VOLPY SPECIAL

This modified Cassutt Volpy #20 showed up at Reno in 1970 without the proper paperwork on wing stress for its new tapered wing, and was disqualified. Later it had several names such as "Spooky," "Trick Chick," #12, "Wrolstad Special" (Tom Wrolstad of Molalla, OR) and "Beginners Luck." In 1994 Fary James of Weathersford, TX was rebuilding it.

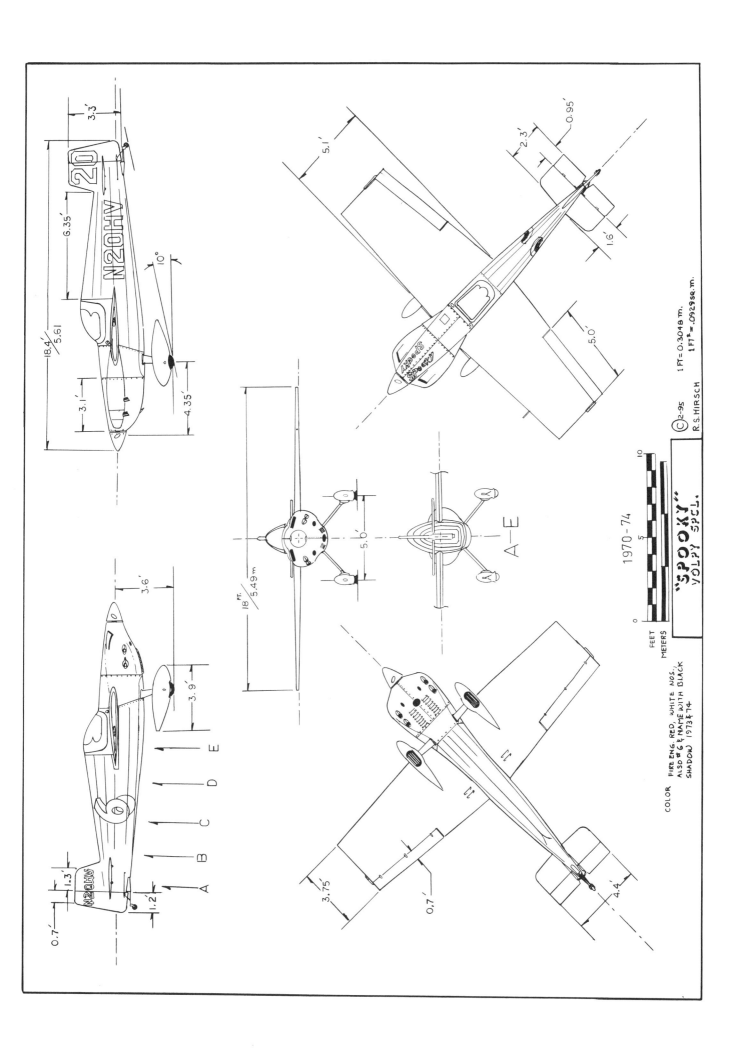

3.3'

6.35'
5.61

18.4'

N20HV

N20HV

10°

3.1'

4.35'

5.1

2.3'

0.95'

1.6'

5.0'

Spooky

3.6'

3.9'

18 FT.
5.49 m

5.0'

A—E

N20HV

N20HV

0.7'

1.3'

1.2'

A B C D E

1970-74

FEET
METERS

0   5   10

©2-95   1 FT.= 0.3048 m.
R.S.HIRSCH   1 FT.²= .0929 sq. m.

"SPOOKY"
VOLPY SPCL.

COLOR FIRE ENG. RED, WHITE NOS.,
ALSO # 6 & NAME WITH BLACK
SHADOW 1973 & 74

3.75'

0.7'

4.4'

1971
"Stinger"
Al Williams

Al Williams who designed and built #34 "Estrellita" for the Goodyear races also designed and built this W-17 "Stinger." John Paul Jones of Granada Hills, CA was the pilot at Point Mugu and Reno in 1971. It placed second in the Consolation race at Reno. The fuselage was metal with wooden wing and tail.

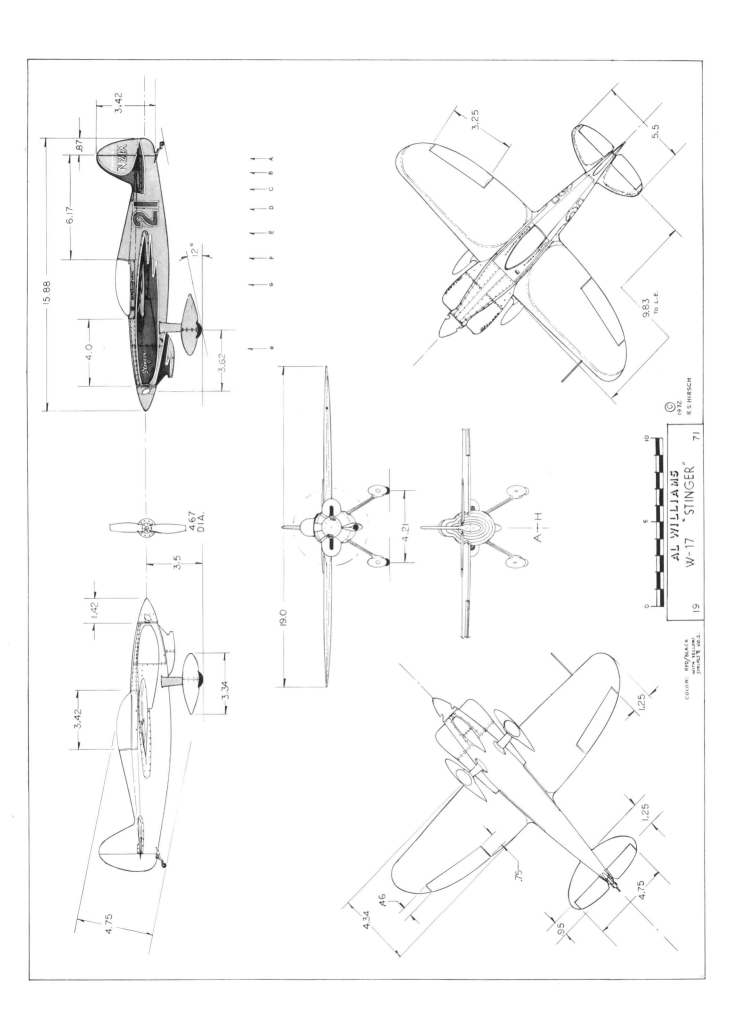

AL WILLIAMS
W-17 "STINGER"

© 1972
R.S. HIRSCH

COLOR: RED/BLACK
WITH YELLOW
STRIPES & NO.S.

19   71

1956-69
"BABY CYCLONE"
JIM WILSON

The Wilson "Baby Cyclone" was built in 1959 and was retired in 1969. It belonged to James H. Wilson and also went under the name of "Snoopy." It was improperly called a Cassutt by race press officials because of its square Cassutt type wing. At Reno it qualified 9th at 162.45 mph and 6th in the Consolation race.

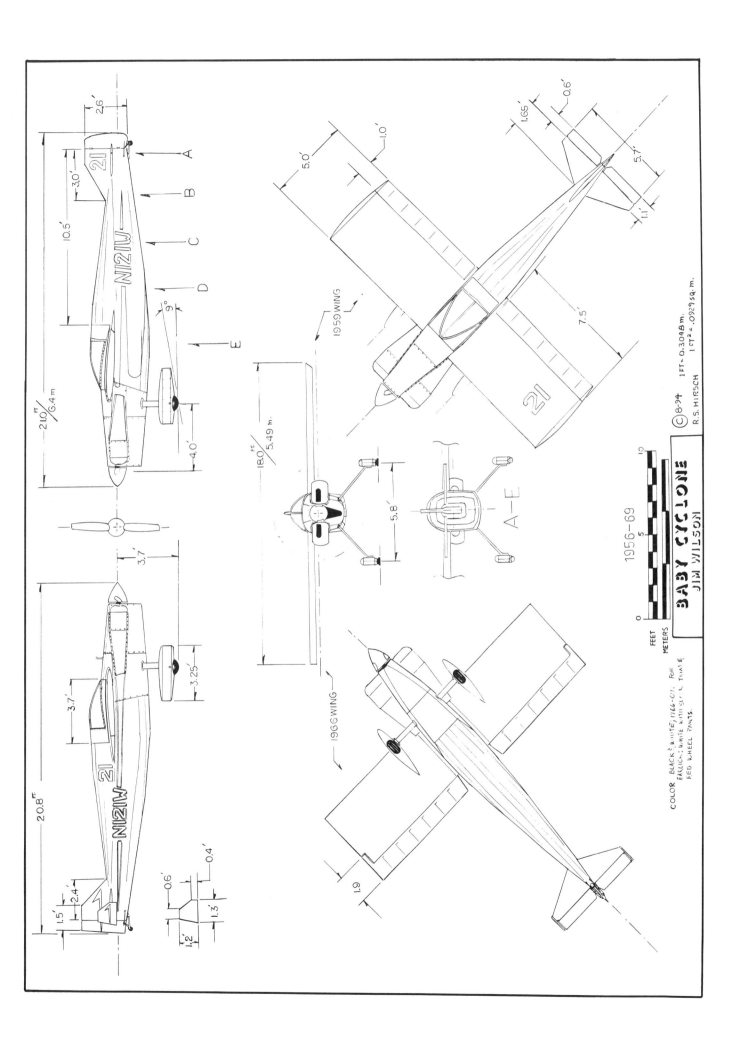

2.6'
3.0'
10.5'
21.0 FT/6.4 m
9°
4.0'
3.7'

A
B
C
D
E

N121W
21

1959 WING

5.0'
1.0'
0.6'
1.65'
5.7'
1.1'
7.5'
21

18.0 FT/5.49 m.

5.8'

A–E

20.8 FT
3.7'
3.25'
1.5'
2.4'
0.6'
0.4'
0.2'
1.3'

N121W
21

1966 WING

1.9'

1956–69

FEET
METERS

10
5
0

BABY CYCLONE
JIM WILSON

COLOR: BLACK & WHITE, 1966–69, FOR
EARLIER - WHITE WITH SILVER & TRIM &
RED WHEEL PANTS.

© 8-94   1 FT = 0.3048 m.   1 FT² = .0929 SQ. m.
R.S. HIRSCH

1971-73
"PLUMB CRAZY"
JIM WILSON

James H. Wilson of Dallas, TX completed his taper-wing Cassutt "Plumb Crazy" in mid 1971 in time for the Cleveland races, and made the finals at both Cleveland and Reno. At Reno that year it turned the fastest time in the section 2-B heats at 203.16 mph, and placed 4th, 0.10 mph behind Nick Jones. In 1972 it qualified at 217.303 mph, and in 1973 it qualified at 215.568 mph. It placed 8th in the Championship race and ran out of gas in a heat race there.

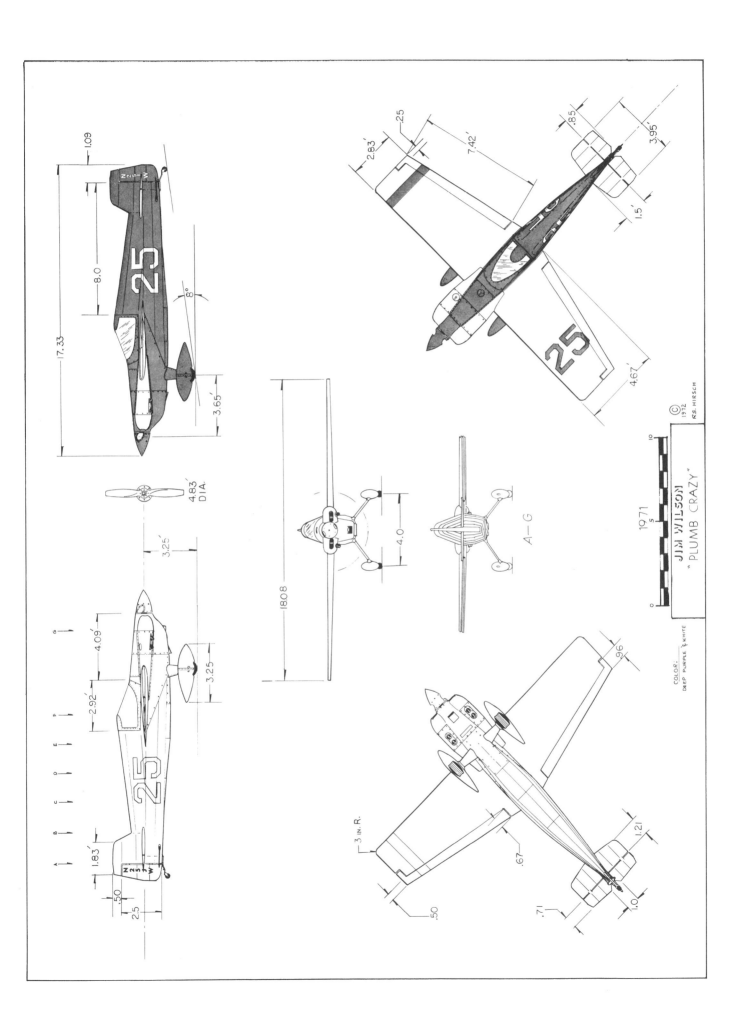

JIM WILSON
"PLUMB CRAZY"

1971

COLOR:
DEEP PURPLE & WHITE

© 1972
R.S. HIRSCH

1983-85
"SUMP'N ELSE"
WH-1

Thomas Summers of Friendship, TX bought back "Thunder Chicken," a Hansen Special WH-1, and raced it at Mojave and Reno from 1978-1984. It was repainted and named "Sump'N Else" for Reno in 1985. It was flown by Ken Haas and later by Tom Cooney. During a heat race while piloted by Jim Dulin, the canopy blew off. "Thunder Chicken" drifted out of the limelight and ended up in the Chino Air Museum.

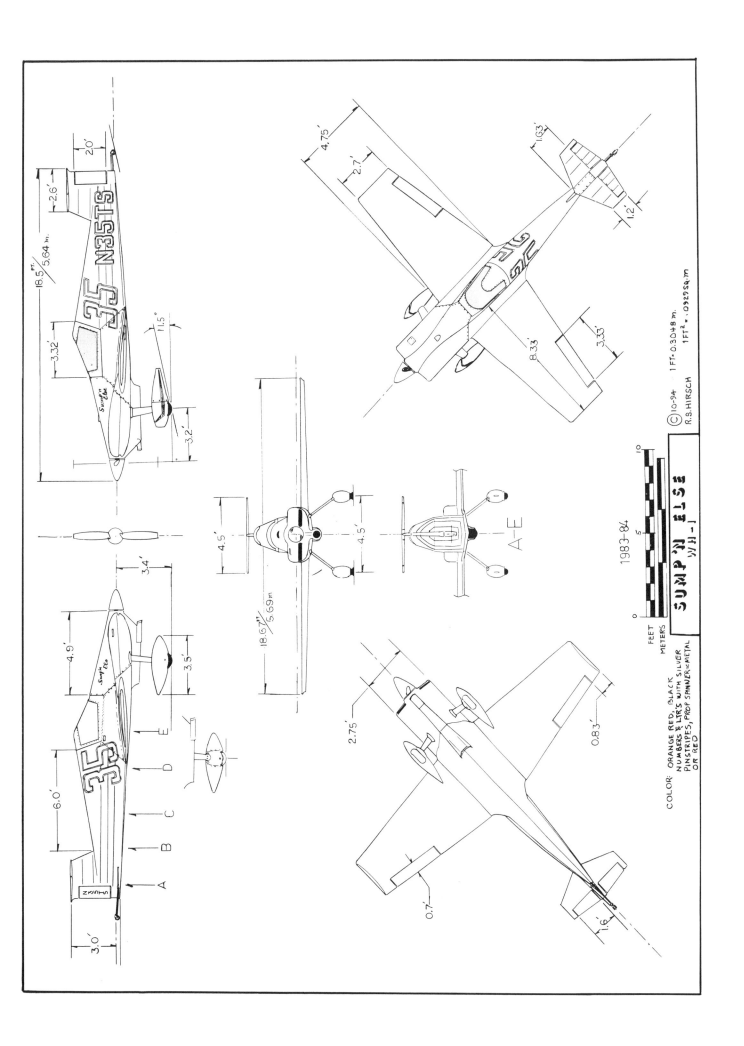

SUMP'N ELSE
JJ H-1

1983-84

COLOR: ORANGE RED, BLACK
NUMBERS & LTR'S WITH SILVER
PINSTRIPES, PROP SPANNER≈METAL
OR RED

© 10-94   1 FT = 0.3048 m.
R.S.HIRSCH   1 FT² = .0929 SQ. m

FEET
METERS

1995
KELLY F-ID

There were two Kelly F-IDs built at the same time. One was sold to Philip Smid and Steve Myers and named "Firefly." It had race number 36. The second became the new "Barbara Jean" with race number 42. The registration number was transferred from the Cassutt after it was retired from racing in 1995. The F-ID #42 was first raced at Reno in 1995 and placed second in the Silver race at 224.334 mph with a non-worked over stock engine. However, the week took its toll, as the engine was burned out. Its fastest lap was 231 mph. It attained 265 mph on straight flight not on the course.

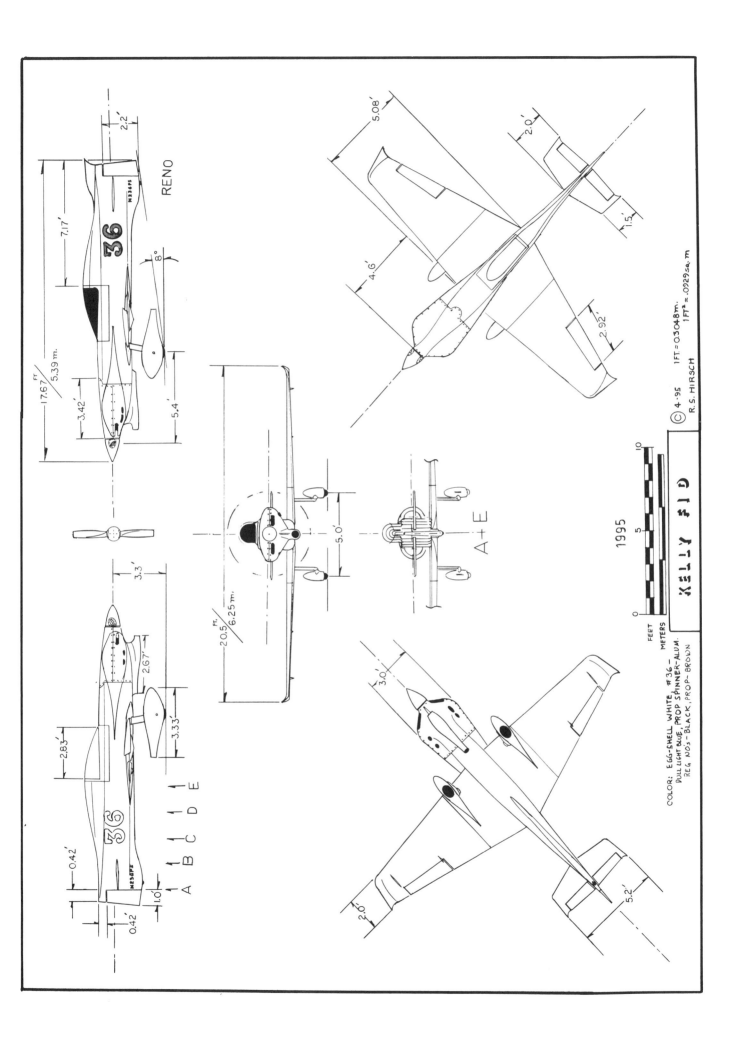

RENO

8°

17.67' / 5.39 m.

7.17'

3.42'

5.4'

2.2'

N236PS

36

A B C D E

2.83'

2.67'

3.3'

3.33'

0.42'

0.42

1.0'

N236PS

36

20.5' Ft. / 6.25 m.

5.0'

A + E

5.08'

4.6'

2.0'

1.5'

2.92'

3.0'

2.0'

5.2'

1995

10

5

0

FEET

METERS

© 4-95   1 FT. = 0.3048 m.
R. S. HIRSCH   1 FT.² = .0929 sq. m

KELLY FLD

COLOR: EGG-SHELL WHITE, #36 —
DULL LIGHT BLUE, PROP SPINNER-ALUM.
REG NOS — BLACK, PROP-BROWN

1974-84
"FLYING DUTCHMAN"

Eldon Lutz of Ogden, UT raced the LDF-3 at Reno in 1973 and at Mojave in 1976. Then Mike Leoning of Boise, ID raced it at Reno in 1976 and qualified at 201.117 mph, but he jumped the gun in the Silver race and was disqualified. Tom Aslett of Twin Falls, ID raced it at Reno in 1981 and 1992. In 1987 it was raced by Lori Love. It showed up at the Phoenix 500 with Lutz as LDF-4 painted all white. It was at Reno in 1995 with Holbrook Maslen of Carson City, NV as the owner/pilot. Larry Love also has piloted this racer.

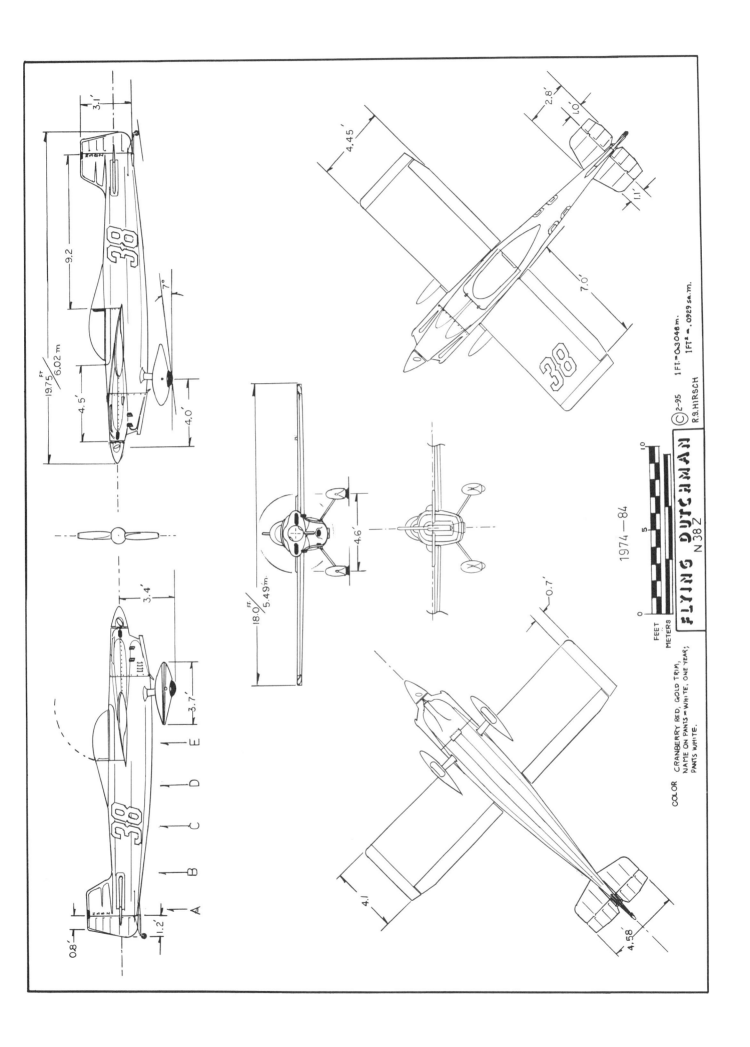

FLYING DUTCHMAN
N38Z

1974—84

COLOR   CRANBERRY RED, GOLD TRIM,
NAME ON PANTS = WHITE, ONE YEAR;
PANTS WHITE.

© 2-95   1 FT.= O.3048 m.   1 FT² = .0929 sa. m.
R.S. HIRSCH

FEET
METERS

1970
"El Bandito"
Sleek Frenzel

This CA-5 Cathaway Special "El Bandito" was designed and partially built by Russell Cathaway. It was sold to a Mr. Frenzel who finished the construction. It was brought to Reno to race in 1968 by Bobby Budde of Morgan Hill, CA. It was yellow, then white and later red with gold trim and numbers. It has been flying and racing for 30 years. The engine cowling change was done in 1995.

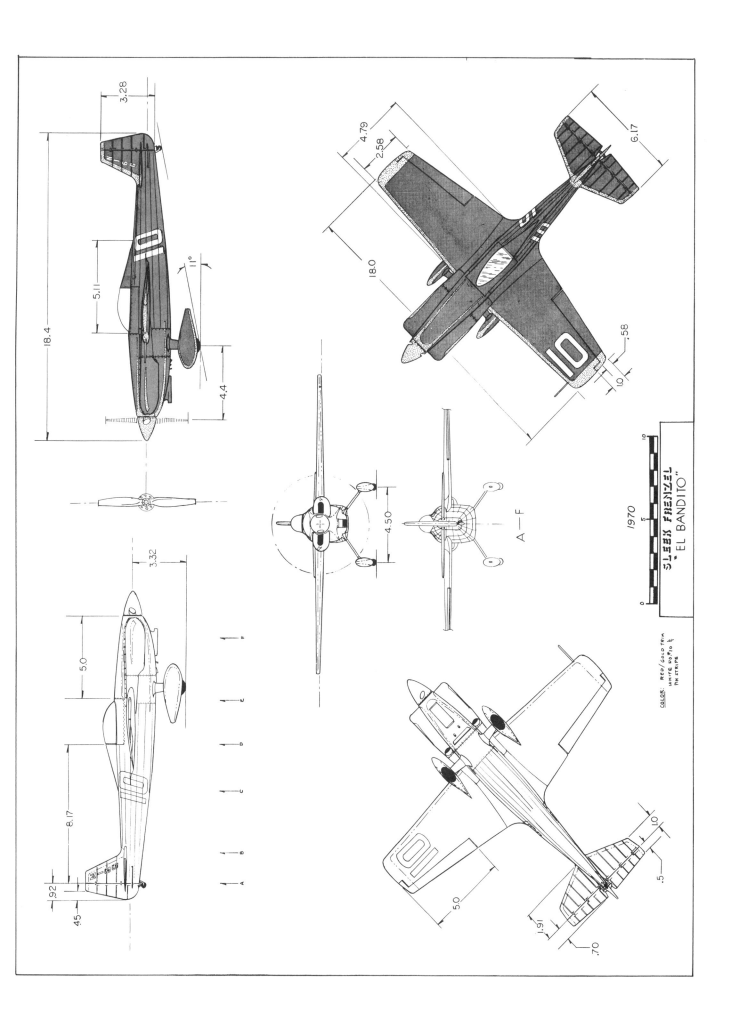

SLEEK FRENZEL "EL BANDITO"

1970

A — F

COLOR: RED/GOLD TRIM
WHITE W.O.⁴⁄₁₀ &
PIN STRIPE

"SHARK"
HARVEY MACE
R-2

Right after the 1966 Reno races Harvey Mace started designing the "Shark" to be ready for the 1970 races. Mace had built the midget Macerschmitt in eight months. The Mace R-2 was all wood and was first flown September 3, 1970, two weeks before Reno qualifications. It weighed 540 pounds and qualified at 198.53 mph, 11th fastest in a field of 24. Mace was the pilot and placed second in the Silver race. It did not show in 1971 since Mace sold it to a Roy Berry who was killed in a light airplane crash, and the racer was tied up in estate actions. In 1973 Col. William L. Skiar of Edward AFB bought it. In 1970 Mace's crew was his wife and two sons. He sold it to buy a boat.

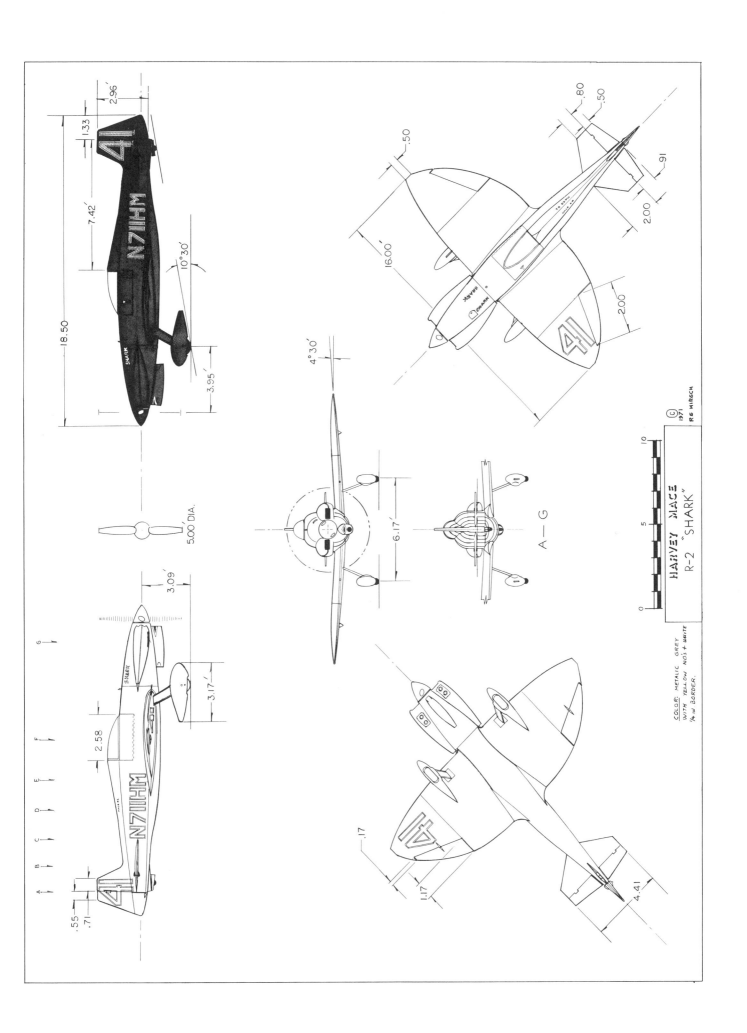

HARVEY MACE
R-2 "SHARK"

COLOR: METALIC GREY
WITH YELLOW NO'S + WHITE
¼ IN BORDER.

© 1971 R G HIRSCH

A — G

1993
"FANDANGO"
MADELAINE KENNY

"Fandango" showed up at Reno in 1992 with Madelaine Kenny of San Carlos, CA as the owner/pilot. It was a modified Cassutt. Her qualifying speed was 188.517 mph. In 1993 she qualified at only 187.005 mph, but then Dave Morss assisted her and she did 191.047 mph, placing second in heat 1-C, and then third in the Bronze race at 185.017 mph. Morss also flew "Fandango" in 1994 at Reno in heat 1-C and did 187.271 mph, placing fourth. Kenny qualified it at 206.530 mph and placed third at 184.249 mph in the Bronze race. This was its last year at Reno, as it was a "no show" in 1995.

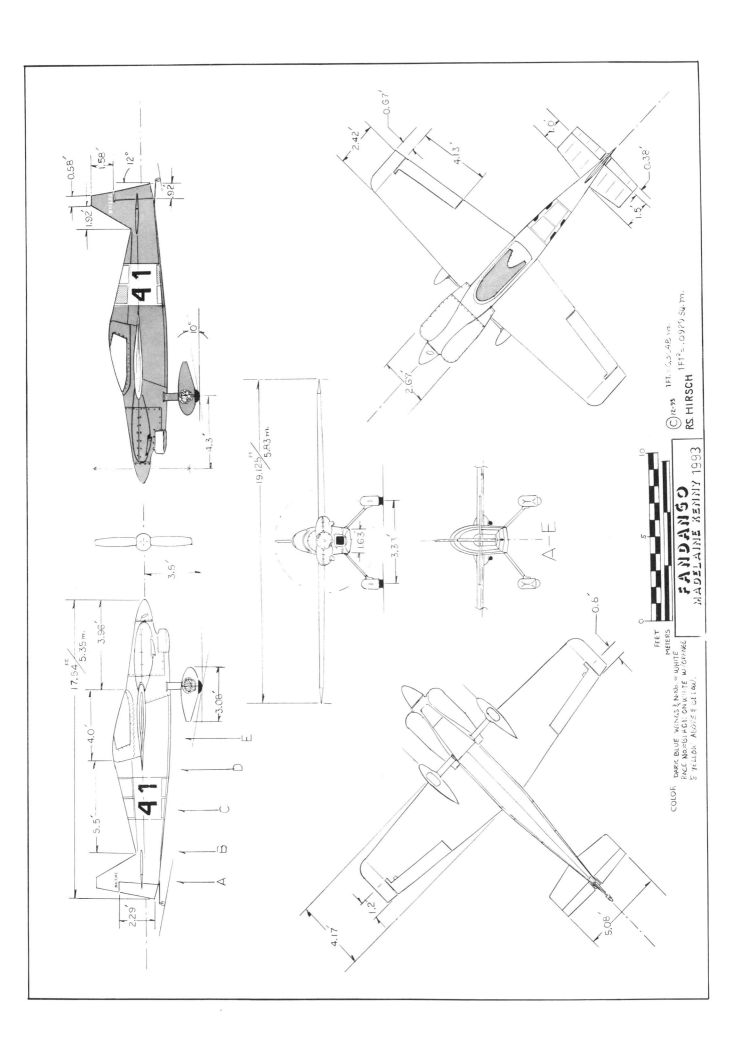

FANDANGO
MADELAINE KENNY 1993

COLOR: DARK BLUE WINGS & N-No. & WHITE
RACE No.-BLACK ON WHITE W/ORANGE
& YELLOW ABOVE & BELOW.

1 FT. = 0.3048 m.
1 FT² = .0929 Sq. m.

© 12-93

19.125 FT / 5.83 m.

17.54 FT / 5.35 m.

3.96'

5.35 m.

A E
B D C

1993-94
"Barbara Jean"

The Kelly CRY original "Barbara Jean" was built in 1986-87 and first flown in 1987. It had 750 hours on it when it came to Reno in 1993. It raced at Reno in 1993 and '94 before being retired to sport plane status. Its maximum speed on the course was 207 to 210 mph. Kelly felt that this was all that could be had from it, and was working on his F-ID design concepts. The name "Barbara Jean" and race number 42 was also on his new F-ID.

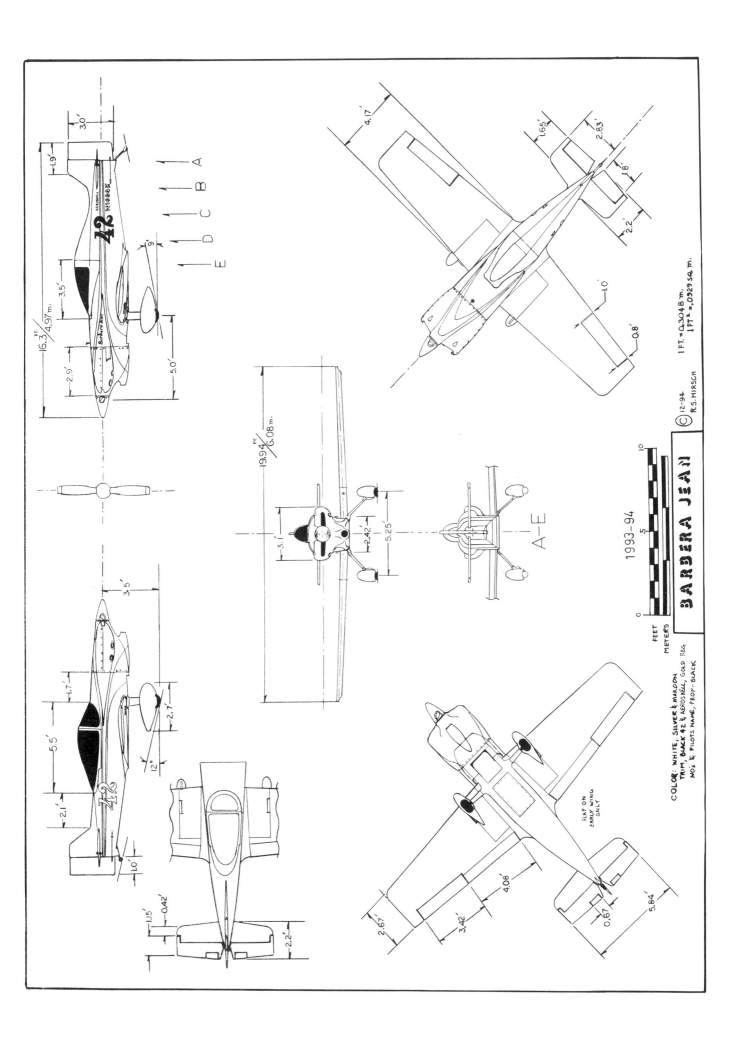

BARBERA JEAN

1993-94

COLOR: WHITE, SILVER & MAROON
TRIM, BLACK 42 & AEROSHELL, GOLD REG.
NO'S & PILOTS NAME; PROP-BLACK

FLAP ON
EARLY WING
ONLY

© 12-94
R.S. HIRSCH

1 FT. = 0.3048 m.
1 FT = .0929 sq. m.

1969-70
"Fey Foo"
Eric Shilling

    "Fey Foo" was built and raced in 1969 by Eric Schilling of El Segundo, CA. It placed fifth in the Consolation race at Reno. "Fey Foo" means "Flying Tigers" in Chinese. It was bought by Ken Haas in 1970 and brought to Reno with the name changed to "Lil Misty." He placed 12th in the time trials and 4th in heat 1-B, then 8th in the Championship race.

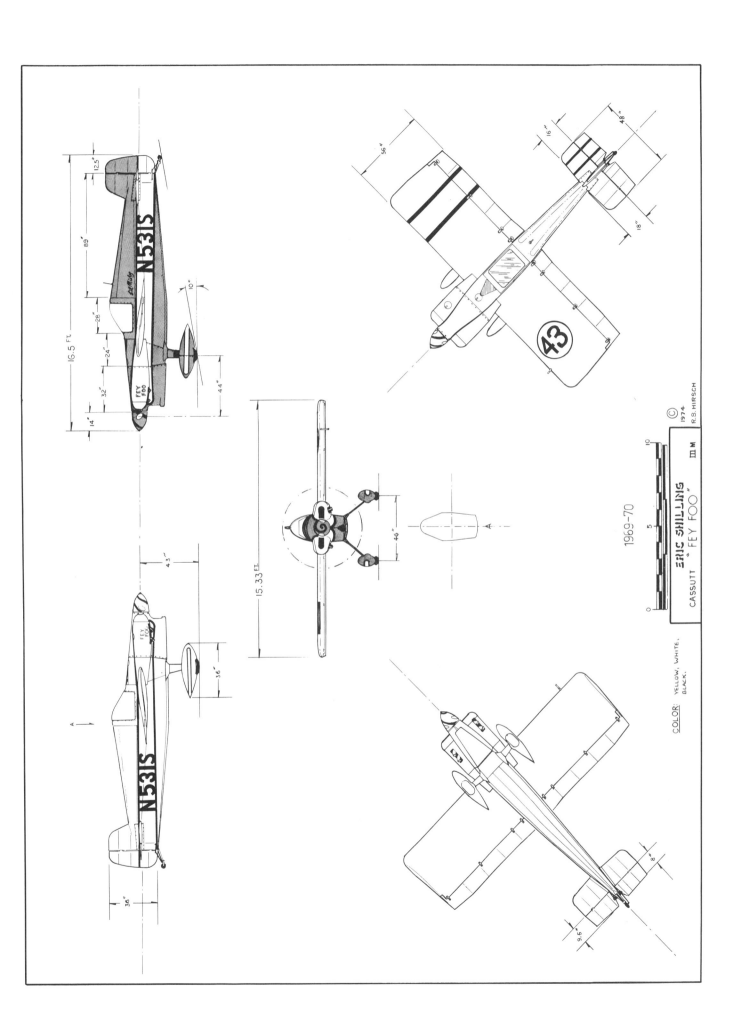

N531S

12.5"
89"
28"
24"
10°
16.5 FT.
32"
14"
FEY FOO
44"

56"
16"
48"
18"

43

4.3"
15.33 FT.
36"

46"

A

8"
9.5"

36"

FEY FOO

1969-70

10
5
0

ⒸR.S. HIRSCH
1974

ERIC SHILLING
CASSUTT "FEY FOO" IIIM

COLOR: YELLOW, WHITE,
BLACK.

"LIL MISTY I"
KENN HAAS

"Lil Misty" was brought to Reno by Kenn Haas of Thousand Oaks, CA with a new wing and his name on the wing panels. It was designated "Misty I" while flown at Point Mugu and "Lil Misty" at Reno in 1970, and qualified at Reno at 195.652 mph. In 1971 it showed up at Cleveland but didn't qualify. It was not at Reno in 1971, but was there in 1972 and qualified 16th at 191.829 mph and placed second in the Medallion race.

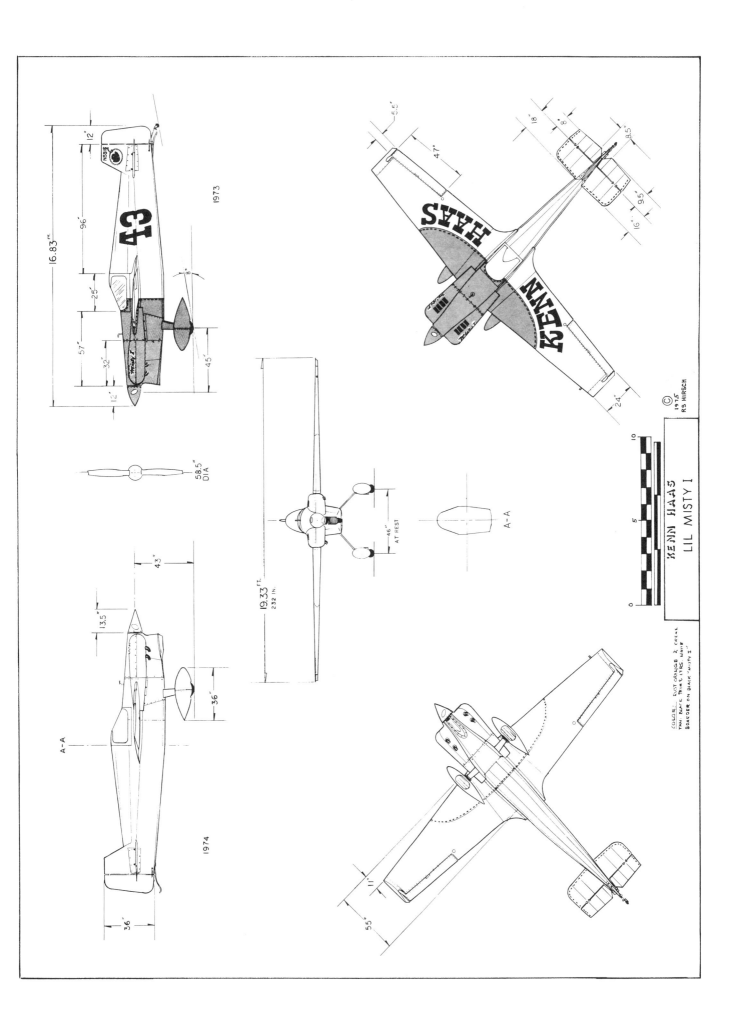

1973

16.83 FT.

12°
96"
25"
57"
32"
12°
8°
45'

N35SI

43

Misty I

58.5"
DIA

A-A

43"
13.5
36"

36"

1974

19.33 FT.
232 IN.

46"
AT REST

A-A

5.5°
18°
8°
8.5"
47"
16"
9.5"
24"

HAAS

KENN

© 1975
R5 HIRSCH

KENN HAAS
LIL MISTY I

0 5 10

COLOR: RUST ORANGE & CREAM
TRAIL PLACE TRIM & LTRS. WHITE
BOARDER ON BLACK "MISTY I"

11"
55°

"SOLUTION"
JUDY WAGNER

    In 1969 at Cleveland Judy Wagner raced in the ten lap 2½-mile course Stock Plane Race and won at 197.46 mph. She then showed up at Cleveland in 1971 with "Solution" and qualified 18th down at 174.08 mph and 11th down at Reno with 208.49 mph, and won the Silver race. She did not show in 1972 but in 1973 at Reno she again qualified 11th down and won the Consolation race. In 1976 at Mojave she qualified at 238.126, second only to Ray Cote. From this point on, Wagner's "Solution" has been one of the "Who's Who" of Formula One racing. Judy and her husband were killed in a private aircraft, and Alan Preston had the now-named "Sitting Duck" up for sale in 1989 for $45,000. It was still racing in 1995 by Thomas Hauptman and named "Jody."

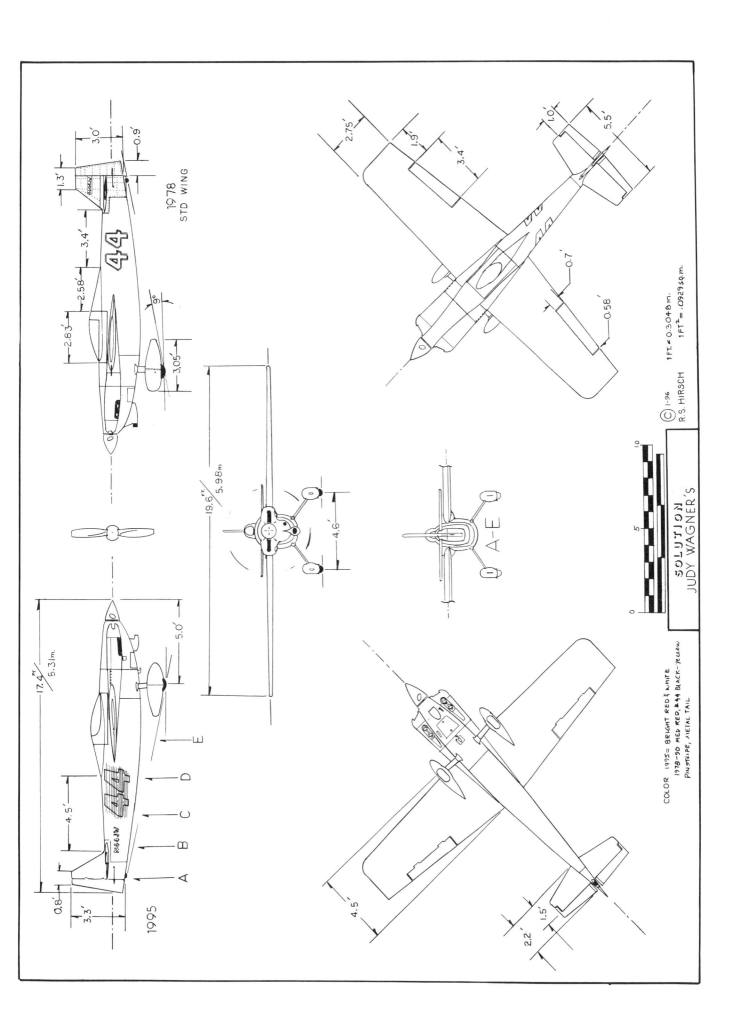

1978
STD WING

1995

SOLUTION
JUDY WAGNER'S

COLOR 1995 = BRIGHT RED & WHITE
1978-90 MED RED, #44 BLACK~YELLOW
PINSTRIPE, METAL TAIL

© 1-96
R.S. HIRSCH

1 FT. = 0.3048 m.
1 FT² = .0929 SQ.m.

"BUMMER'S BULLET"
JIM BUMFORD

Jim Bumford brought this all-composite IFM to Reno in 1988. It was designed by Robbie Grove of San Diego and called a GR-7. It had a high aspect ratio wing for reduced drag on the turns. Its race number was 55 and it was named "Bummer's Bullet." A second GR-7 named "Blue Streak" with number 96 was flown by Jon Sharp and was the 1989 top qualifier at 242.548 mph at Reno. #55 with Jim Bumford did 237.603 mph. #96 was flown by Daniel Gray, an airline pilot from Encino, CA. From 1990 through 1993, #55 was flown by Bill Larson of Edmond, OK. It was sold to a Greg Riddle and Eric Matheson, and on a test flight was destroyed in a fatal crash at the French Valley Airport in Murietta, CA killing 1st Lt. Gregory Riddle. #96 was still racing in 1994 and '95 piloted by Katherine Gray. It had been renamed "Geronimo."

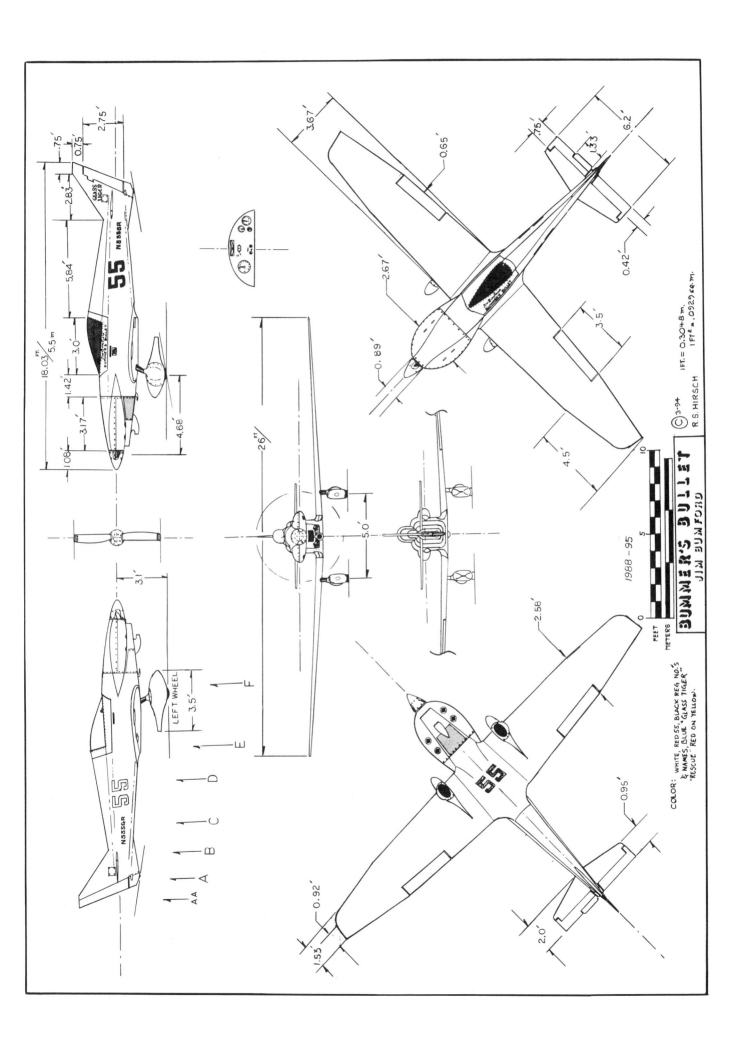

BUMMER'S BULLET

JIM BUMFORD

1988 - 95

© 3-94   1 FT. = 0.3048 m.   1 FT² = .0929 sq. m.
R.S. HIRSCH

COLOR: WHITE, RED 55, BLACK REG NO.5
& NAMES, BLUE "GLASS TIGER"
"RESCUE" RED ON YELLOW.

LEFT WHEEL

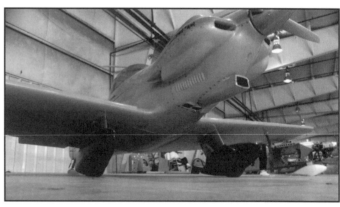

In 1988 Rick Todd built "Titch N' Ash" which was designed by John Taylor. It appeared at Reno and placed 7th in the Bronze race at 155.987 mph. It qualified at 169.247 mph and was 5th in heat 1-C. In 1989 it qualified at 180.610 mph but placed last in heat 1-C at 169.424, 14 mph faster than in 1988, but then the whole field was getting faster. Rick qualified #56 in 1990 at 176.315 mph, and placed last again in heat 1-C. He did 171.320 mph for 5th place in heat 2-C. Rick eventually put this racer up for sale, and as of 1995 it was still in a hangar at Georgetown, CA. Rick now flies a Cassutt #57.

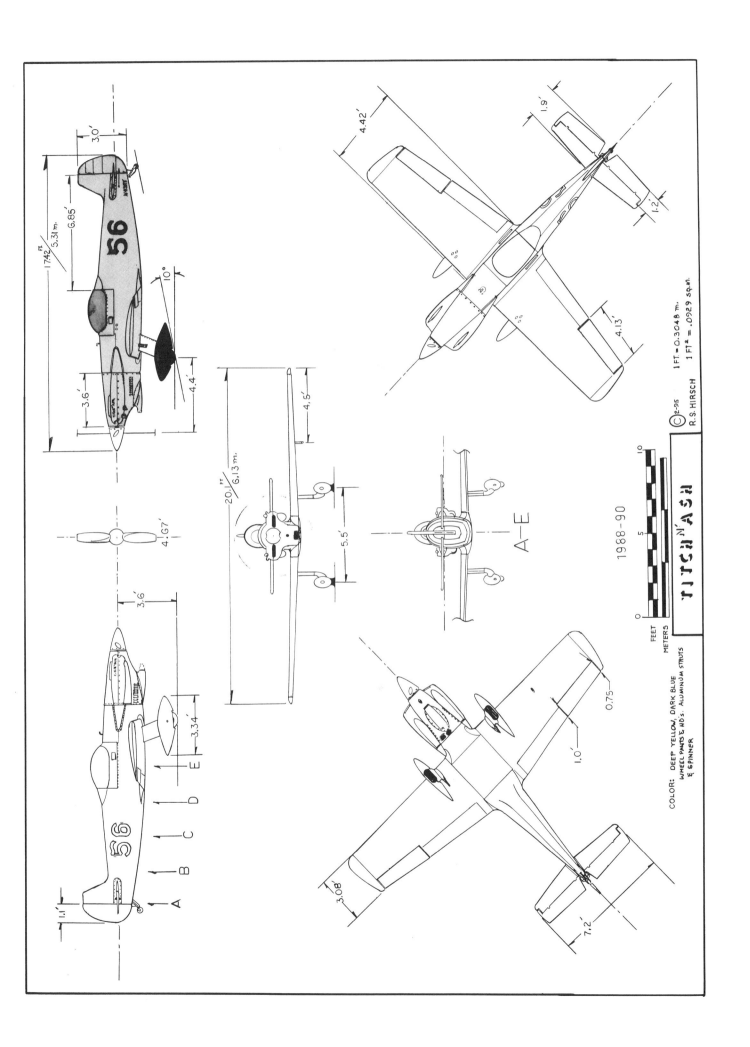

3.0'

1742 FT
5.31 m.

6.85'

10°

3.6'   4.4'

4.67'

3.6'

3.34'

E
D
C
B
A

1.1'

20.1 FT
6.13 m.

4.5'

5.5'

A-E

4.42'   1.9'

1.2'

4.13'

3.08'   7.2'

1.0'

0.75'

1988-90

TITCH'ASH

10

5

FEET
METERS
0

© 2-95
R. S. HIRSCH

1 FT = 0.3048 m.
1 FT² = .0929 SQ.M.

COLOR: DEEP YELLOW, DARK BLUE
WHEEL PANTS ENDS, ALUMINUM STRUTS
& SPINNER

1964-69
"LIL HONEY"
DENNIS POLEN

The Polen Special "Lil Honey" was built by Dennis Polen of Oregon in 1964. It was brought to Reno in 1968 and '69 but never raced. It was used mostly as a private plane by Dennis, who built up about 400 hours in it before selling it. He built a more powerful plane, one with retractable gear and controllable propeller using a Midget Mustang fuselage from the cockpit aft.

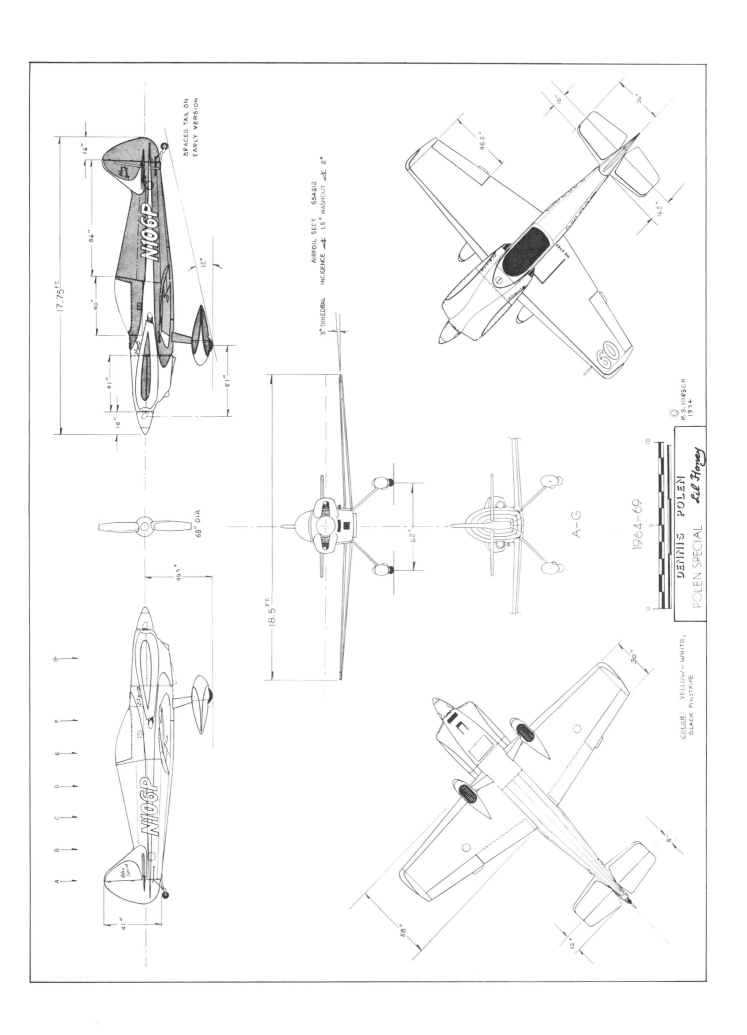

BRACED TAIL ON EARLY VERSION

16"
86"
40"
17.75 FT.
41"
51"
16"

12°

AIRFOIL SECT 65A212
INCIDENCE ∡ 1.5° WASHOUT ∡ 2°

3° DIHEDRAL

68" DIA

49.5"

18.5 FT.

62"

A-G

46.5"

10"
36"
16.5"

NO STEP

60

30"
58"
8"
12"

41"

A B C D E F G

1964-69

DENNIS POLEN *Lil Honey*

POLEN SPECIAL

0 5 10

© R. S. HIRSCH 1974

COLOR: YELLOW-WHITE, BLACK PINSTRIPE

1968-70
"Miss San Bernardino"
E.E. Stover

"Miss San Bernardino" is the cleaned up "Skeeter." Work was done by Art Scholl and San Bernardino College students in 1962. It was also at one time called "La Jollita." Lawrence A. Borrow of Phoenix, AZ tried to qualify it at Reno but damaged two propellers, one engine, a landing gear, root faring and wheel pants in two landing attempts. The owner was Eugene E. Stover who had Art Scholl qualify it. In 1980 it showed up at Reno as #9 "Little Niner" with Marshall Wells of Grants Pass, OR. Larry D. Lowe of Mesa, CA raced it at Mojave. It was also owned by Bill Hauprich and named "Zorp."

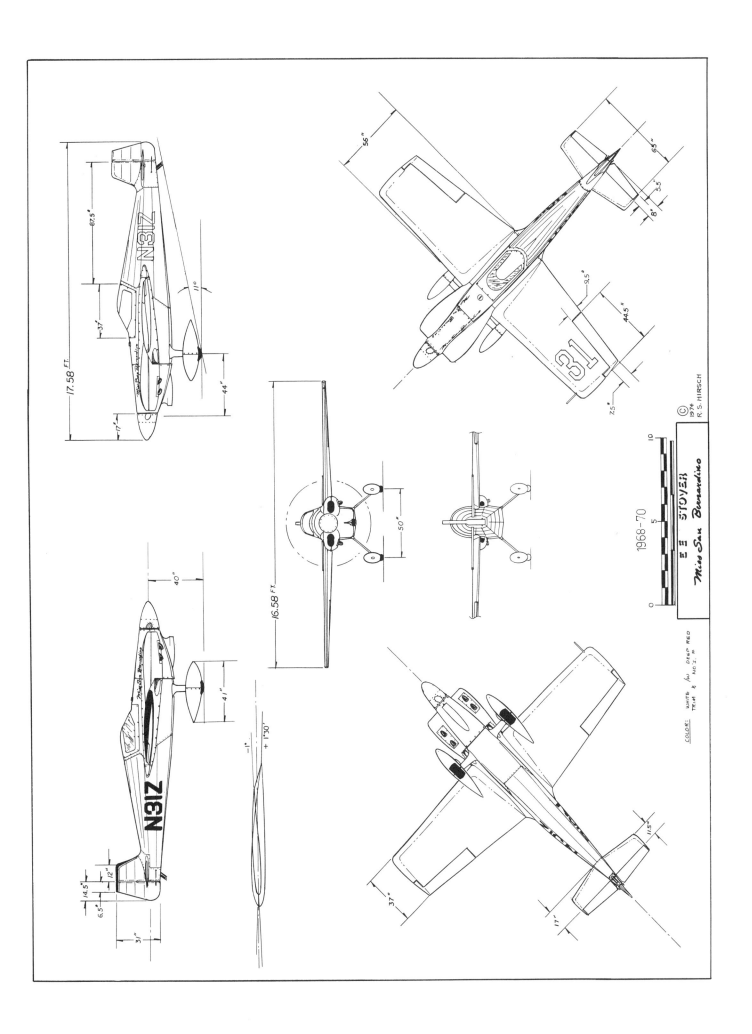

N31Z

17.58 FT.

87.5"

37"

11°

44"

17"

N31Z

40"

41"

14.5"
12"
6.5"
31"

16.58 FT.

-1°
+1°30'

50"

56"

65"

5.5"
8"

9.5"

44.5"

7.5"

31

115"

37"

17"

1968-70

E E STOVER
Miss San Bernardino

COLOR: WHITE b/w DEEP RED
TRIM & NO. 1.71

© 1974
R. S. HIRSCH

0   5   10

1990-94
"Chico Puro"
Alberto Rossi

"Chico Puro" is a modified Cassutt flown by Alberto Rossi of Palo Alto, CA. It raced with number 62 in 1990 and '91, and qualified in 1990 at Reno at 185.610 mph. In 1991 at Reno it pulled out of heat 2-A but did 203.972 mph finishing 7th in the Silver race. In 1993 it qualified 9th down at 222.983 mph and placed third in the Gold race at 236.785 mph at Reno.

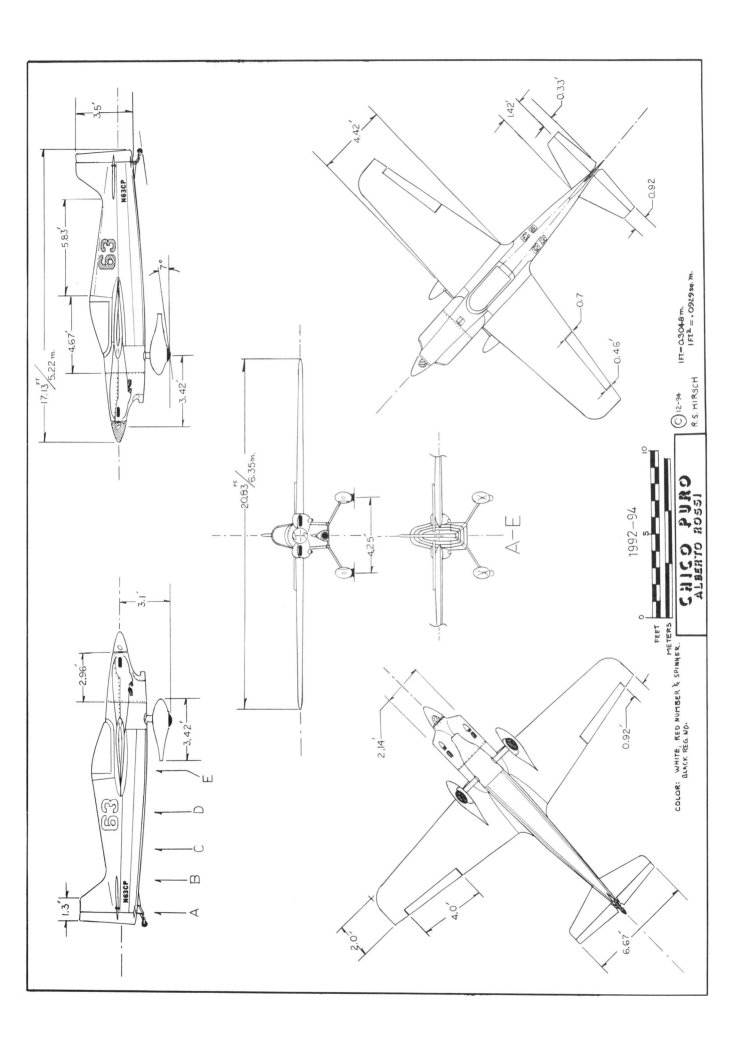

CHICO PURO
ALBERTO ROSSI

1992-94

© 12-94
R.S. HIRSCH

1 FT.= 0.3048 m.
1 FT.² = .0929 sq. m.

COLOR: WHITE, RED NUMBER & SPINNER.
BLACK REG. NO.

FEET
METERS

N63CP

A-E

"IDJITS MIDGET"
JACK LOWERS
R-1

    "Idjits Midget" was built in 1967 by Jack Lowers of Clinton, NC who claimed he did not use Cassutt drawings. It raced at Cleveland placing 4th in the Consolation race in 1967. It was the only wire-braced racer in 1968. It was sold to Nelson Andrews Aircraft Co. in Charleston, WV and placed third in the St. Louis and Reno consolation races. At the Federick races in 1968 it qualified at 197.69 mph and did 201.12 mph for 3rd place in heat 2-B. It was renamed "Moonshiner" at Reno in 1969. At the Miami Nationals from April 16th through 19th in 1969 it qualified at 213.39 mph and placed 5th in the Gold race at 206.92 mph. It had a midair collision in June of 1972 at the Dallas races killing Hugh Alexander in #70 "Bennetts Majic" It was rebuilt after the accident and raced at Miami, Evansville and Fort Wayne. Chuck Andrews crashed "Moonshiner" one week before the 1987 Reno races.

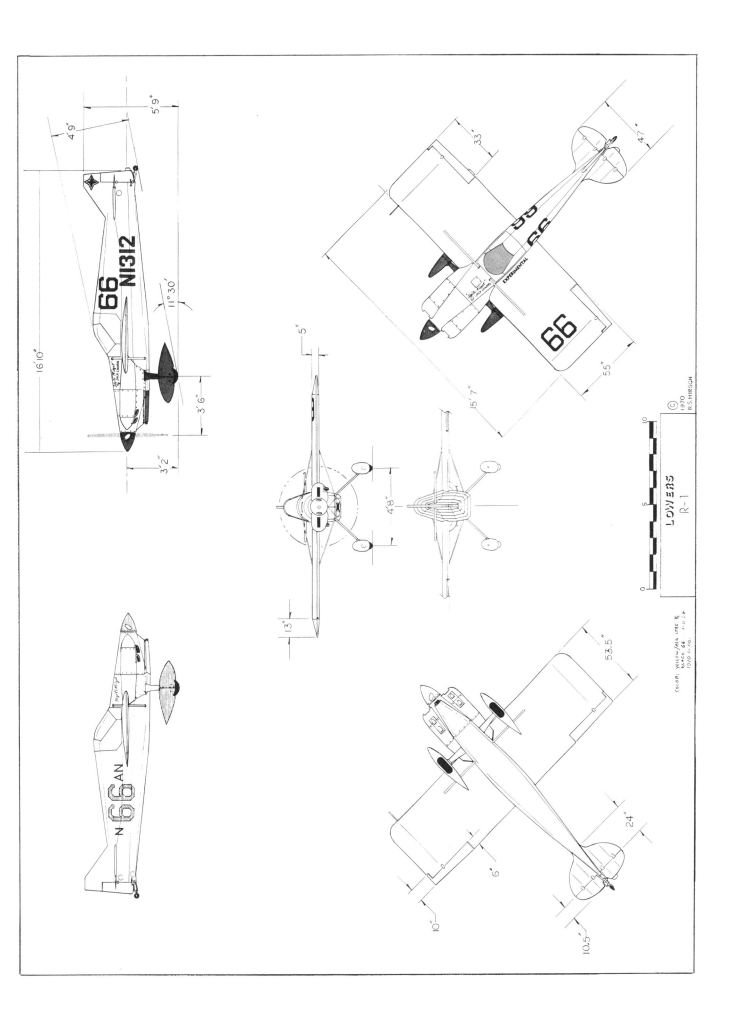

5'9"
4'9"
66 N1312
16'0"
11° 30'
3'6"
3'2"

33
47'
66
EXPERIMENTAL
66
15'7"
5.5"

5"
4'8"
13"

© 1970 R.S. HIRSGH

LOWERS
R-1

COLOR: YELLOW/RED LTRE
BLACK 66
1910 KING

N66 AN

53.5"
24"
6'
10"
10.5'

1949-69
"DEERFLY"
MIKE ARGANDER

"Deerfly" was a complete new design, although there are similarities between the two planes. Keith Sorenson of La Crescenta and Burbank, CA and Mike Argander of Eagle Rock, CA built this one called "Argander Special." It was only 25% completed when Mike Argander was killed testing one of Art Chester's designs. It sat for a few months before construction was restarted and was finished in 1949. Herman "Fish" Salmon gave some support and it placed second at the 1949 Cleveland races. Bill Stead bought it and flew it at races before the Florida mishap. He changed the race number from 39 to 84 before he was killed in it.

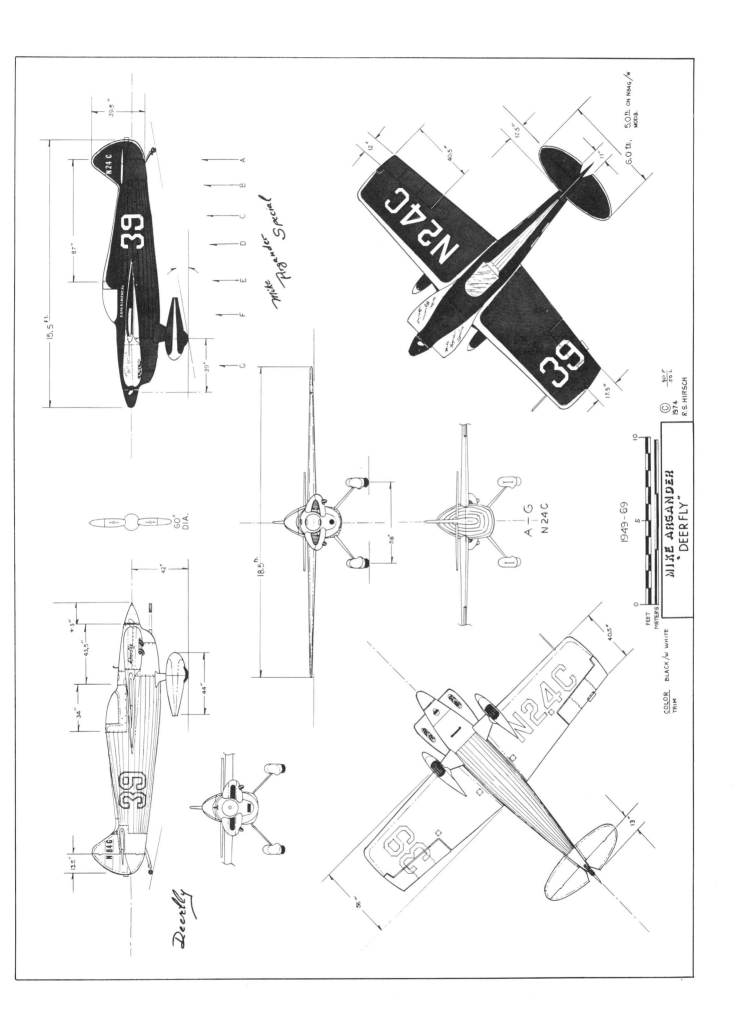

Mike Argander Special

Deerfly

MIKE ARGANDER
"DEERFLY"

1949-69

COLOR   BLACK /w WHITE
TRIM

© 1974
R.S. HIRSCH

1988-89
"VIDEO CASSUTT"
DAVE MORSS

A modified Cassutt "Video Cassutt" built by Dave Morss of San Carlos, CA for the 1987 Reno races. It qualified at 178.622 mph , and in 1988 at 197.391 mph. It was scheduled in heat 1-C but did not start. The pilot was Gary Hubler of Caldwell, ID, placing 4th in the Bronze race. It was up for sale in August 1989 and did not race at Reno. It later became No. 11 owned by Dave Hoover.

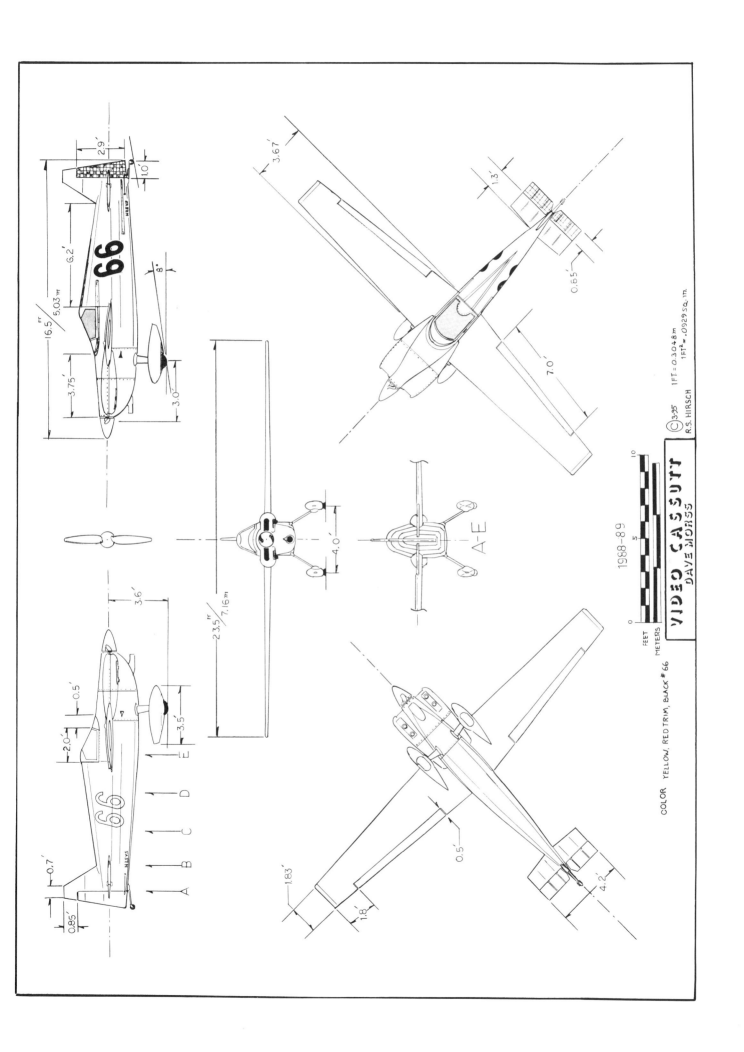

VIDEO CASSUTT
DAVE MORSS

1988-89

COLOR YELLOW, RED TRIM, BLACK #66

©3-95   1 FT = 0.3048 m
R.S. HIRSCH   1 FT² = .0929 SQ. m.

FEET
METERS

1992-94
"MISS RENO"
LAKE TAHOE

"Miss Reno" owned by Don Beck of Incline Village, NV came to Reno in 1990 with a qualifying speed of 225.272 mph. It came back with Roy Channing in 1991 and qualified at 226.319 mph. In 1992 it did 229.332 mph and placed 7th in the Gold. It reached the third highest speed in qualification at 236.602 in 1993 but came in last in the Gold race. It didn't show in 1994. It was built in 1977 and owned by Chuck Wentworth. Its first flight was September 16, 1977. It was also named "Flexi Flyer," "Vomit Comet," "Jaws" and "Passing Fancy," but was somewhat obscure until Reno in 1990 and later.

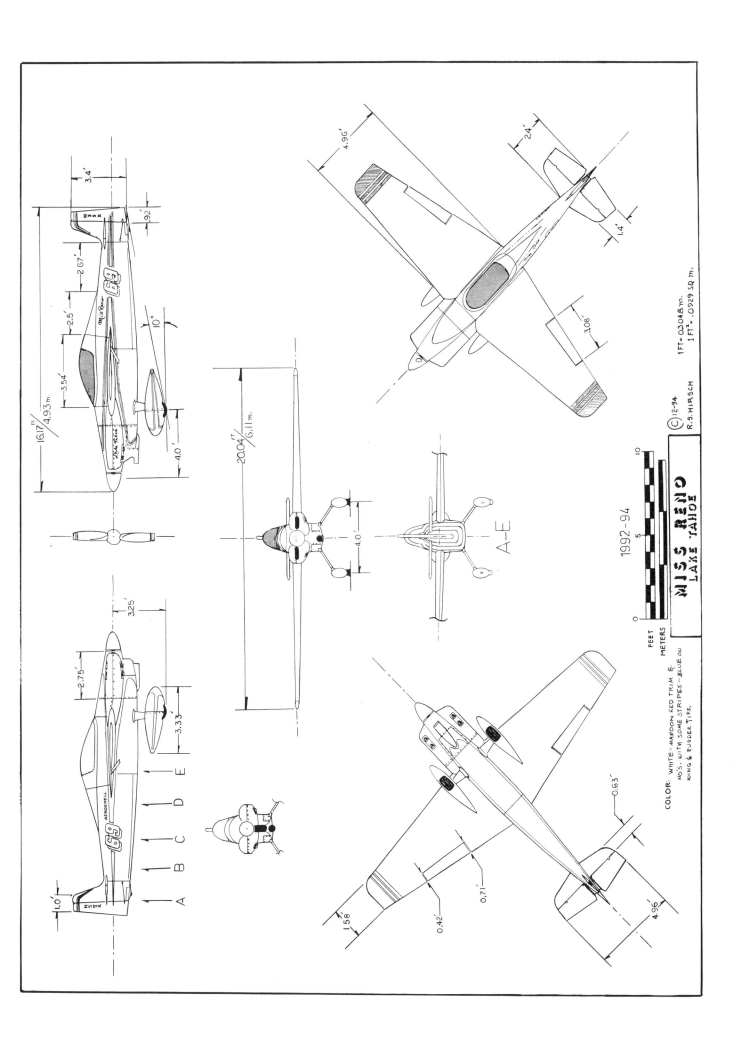

MISS RENO
LAKE TAHOE

1992-94

FEET
METERS

COLOR: WHITE - MAROON RED TRIM &
NO'S. WITH SOME STRIPES - BLUE ON
WING & RUDDER TIPS.

© 12-94
R.S. HIRSCH

1 FT = 0.3048 m.
1 FT² = .0929 SQ m.

1980-83 (1950)
"SKY MOUSE"
TOM WILSON

Tom Wilson of Los Angeles designed and built a second GR-7 design called "Sky Mouse." It was at Claremont in 1950 and was called "Wilson C-J." It only raced three times then but went through some C.G. mods between races. It was not raced for many years but re-surfaced with mods and raced in the early 1980s. There also was an MDR-1 built by M.D. Robinson of High Point, NC that had the same configuration, possibly from the same plans, but this one had not entered racing.

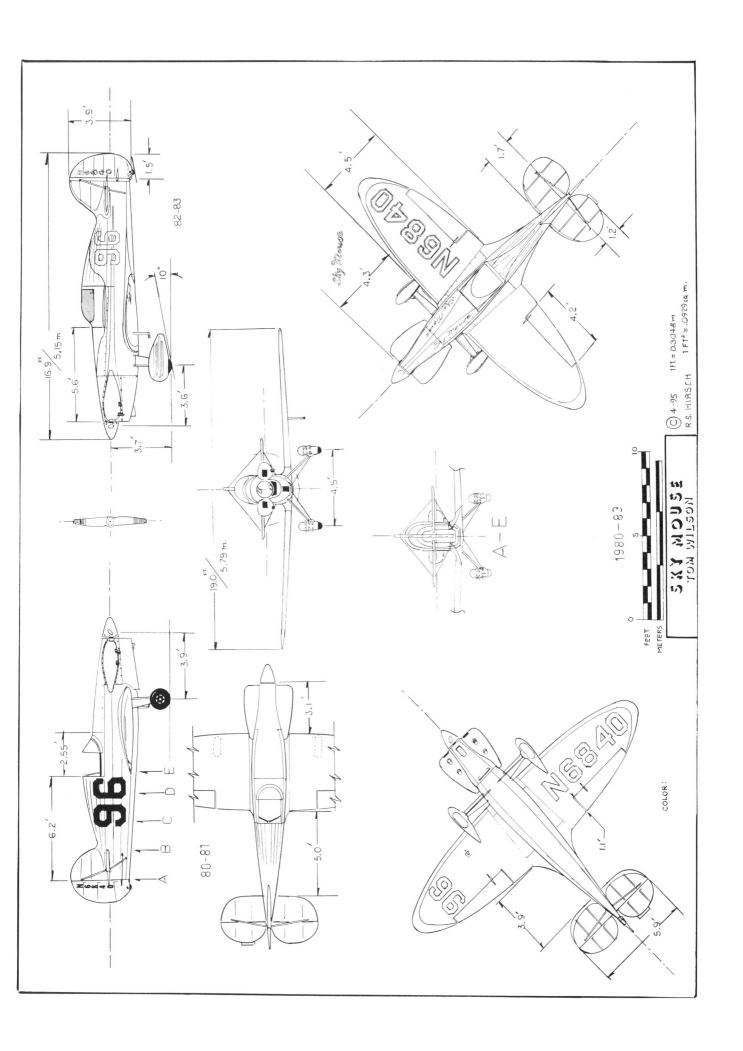

3.9'

1.5'

82-83

10°

16.9' 5.15 m

5.6'

3.6'

3.7'

4.5'

4.3'

4.5'

1.7'

1.2'

4.2'

A-E

1980-83

19.0' 5.79 m.

3.9'

2.55'

6.2'

A B C D E

80-81

3.1'

5.0'

1.1'

3.9'

5.9'

COLOR:

© 4-95   1 FT ≈ 0.3048 m
R.S. HIRSCH   1 FT² ≈ .0929 sq. m.

SKY MOUSE
TOM WILSON

10

5

0

FEET
METERS

1974-75
"Lil Quickie"
Vince DeLuca

Vincent G. DeLuca of Miraleste, CA completed his OR-71 "Lil Quickie" in 1972 and it was test flown on July 9th at the Chino, CA airport. In 1972 it qualified 8th at Reno at 213.861 mph. It was 3rd in heat 2-A at Reno behind "Boo Ray" and "Plumb Crazy" and was 6th in the Gold race behind "Fang." This was the fourth racer built from George Owl's plans. In 1973 at Reno its qualifying speed was 223.602 mph, 5th down, but in heat 1-A it was second behind Ray Cote's "Shoestring" and was 5th in the Gold race. At Mojave, Vince won the Silver race in 1973 at 222.397 mph. Gary Wilson flew it at Reno placing second behind John Parker's "Wild Turkey." Wilson is from Hawaii and named the plane "Aloha." It eventually became No. 4 "Alley Cat" with Bill Ippolito and Ray Cote.

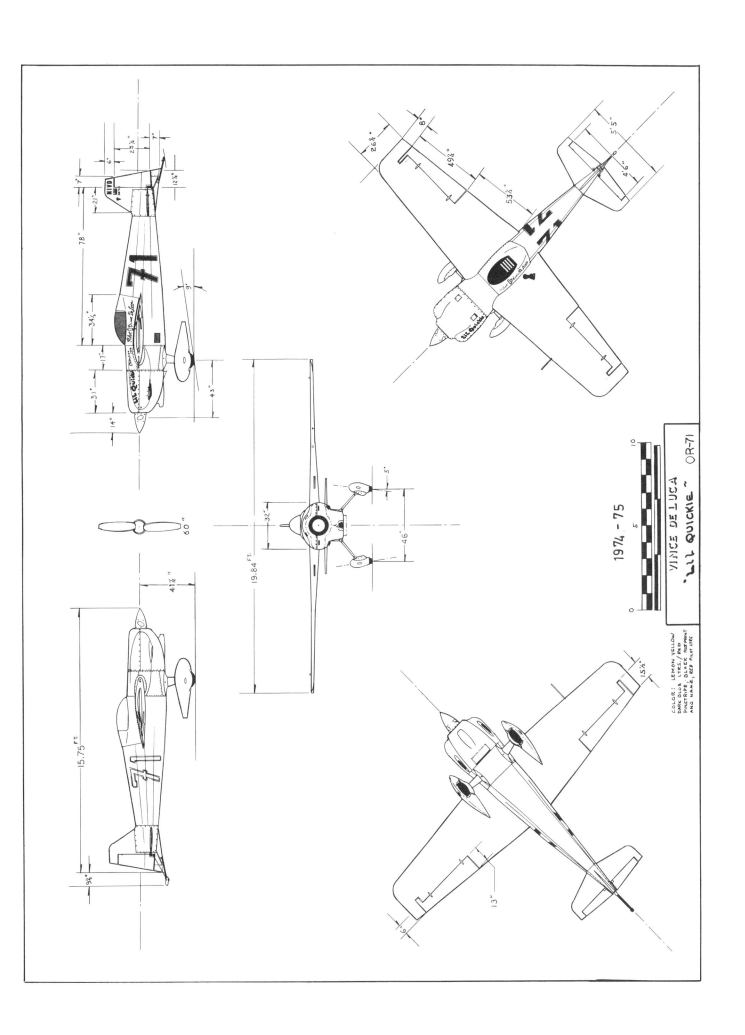

VINCE DE LUCA
"LIL QUICKIE" OR-71

1974 - 75

COLORS: LEMON YELLOW/
DARK BLUE LTRS., RED
PINSTRIPE, BLACK FOOTPRINT
AND NAME, RED PILOT LTRS.

"TOM CAT"
T.A. COONEY

Tom Cooney of Indianapolis built his "Tom Cat" in 1964 and qualified 11th at Reno with a speed of 155.98 mph that year. He placed 5th in the Consolation race. He then went to the Las Vegas races in 1964 and qualified at 160.9 mph and was 4th in the Consolation race. He came back to Reno in 1968 with an 0-200 engine. In 1969 during a ferry flight, he lost power and set it down among trees, wiping out the craft for that period.

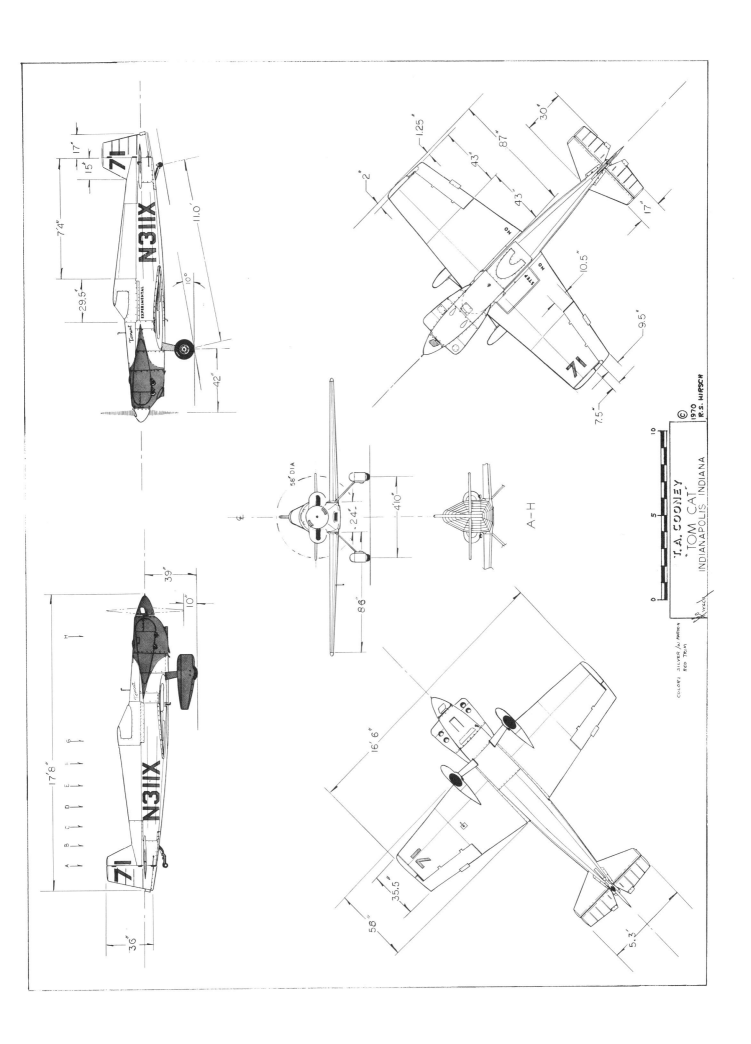

COLOR: SILVER /w/ MAROON
RED TRIM

© 1970 R.S. HIRSCH

T.A. COONEY
"TOM CAT"
INDIANAPOLIS, INDIANA

1973-76
"Texas Gem"
Jim Miller

Jim Miller's JM-2 named "Texas Gem" was built in 1973 and started racing in 1974. Miller was absent from air racing for over a decade but this unusual design contained more original ideas than any other racer in the history of midget racers. It is made of vacuum-formed honeycomb-reinforced fiberglass. The design work began in 1971 and was approved by the FAA in 1972. The rudders were at first segments of the propeller shroud and the elevator was a full-flying surface up front because the canard control corrected the tendency to tuck the nose down on takeoff. Jim built and extensively tested a radio-controlled model for flight characteristics data. The nosewheel was steerable. He had an accident at the Falcon Field races early in 1976 so he rebuilt and modified it into a slimmer configuration with the elevator and rudder on top of the smaller prop-shroud.

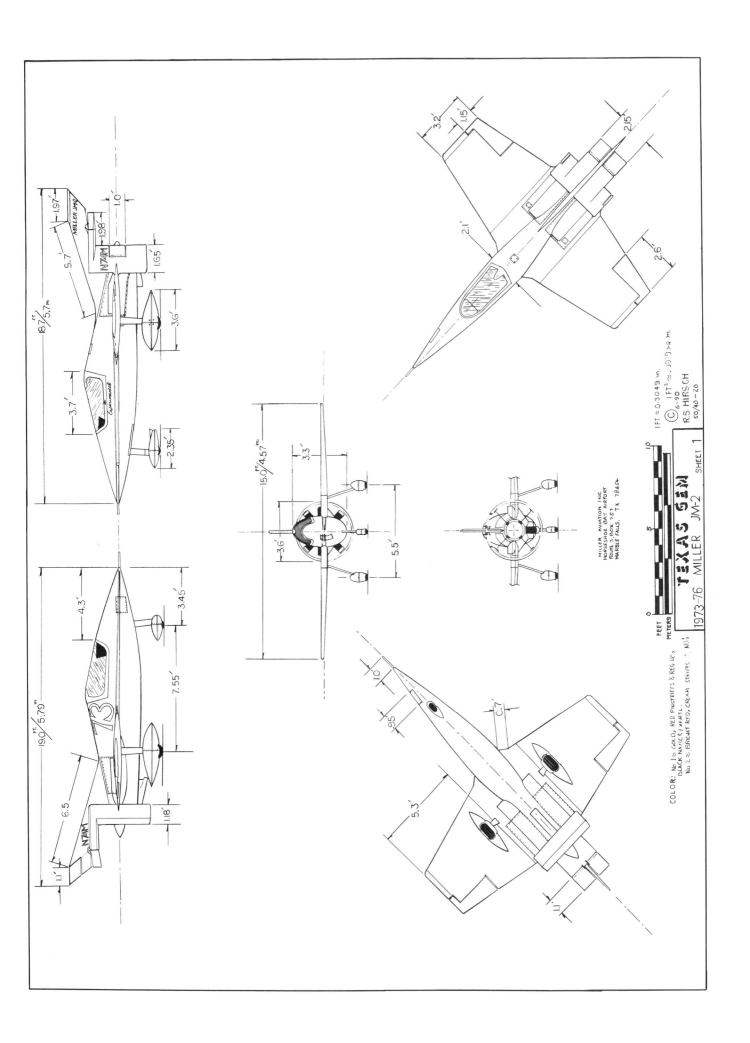

COLOR: No.1 = GOLD, RED PINSTRIPES & REG N°s
         BLACK NAME & PANEL.
         No.2 = BRIGHT RED, CREAM STRIPES & N°s

MILLER AVIATION INC.
HORSESHOE BAY AIRPORT
ROUTE 3, BOX 757
MARBLE FALLS, TX 78654

1 FT ≈ 0.3049 m.
© 6-90   1 FT² ≈ .0919 SQ. m.
R.S. HIRSCH
50/40 ~ 20

TEXAS GEM
1973-76 MILLER JM-2   SHEET 1

FEET 0 5 10
METERS

1987-89
"Texas Gem"
"Puffin"

The "Texas Gem" underwent many changes in 1976 including a retracting nosewheel and a 44-inch two-blade propeller, replacing the four-blade prop. It was painted a bright red instead of the earlier gold. Also the prop-shroud was removed. Jim Miller raced it in 1984 and sold it to Errol Robertson of Warrenton, OR in 1985, and then built his "Pushy Cat." Errol remodeled it after Miller's new racer, and painted it white and renamed it "Puffin." In 1986 it qualified at a speed of 233.639 mph at Reno. Errol, while flying an early heat at Reno in 1989, flew through a dust devil rounding pylon 6, causing the left wing to fold up and the craft just disintegrated.

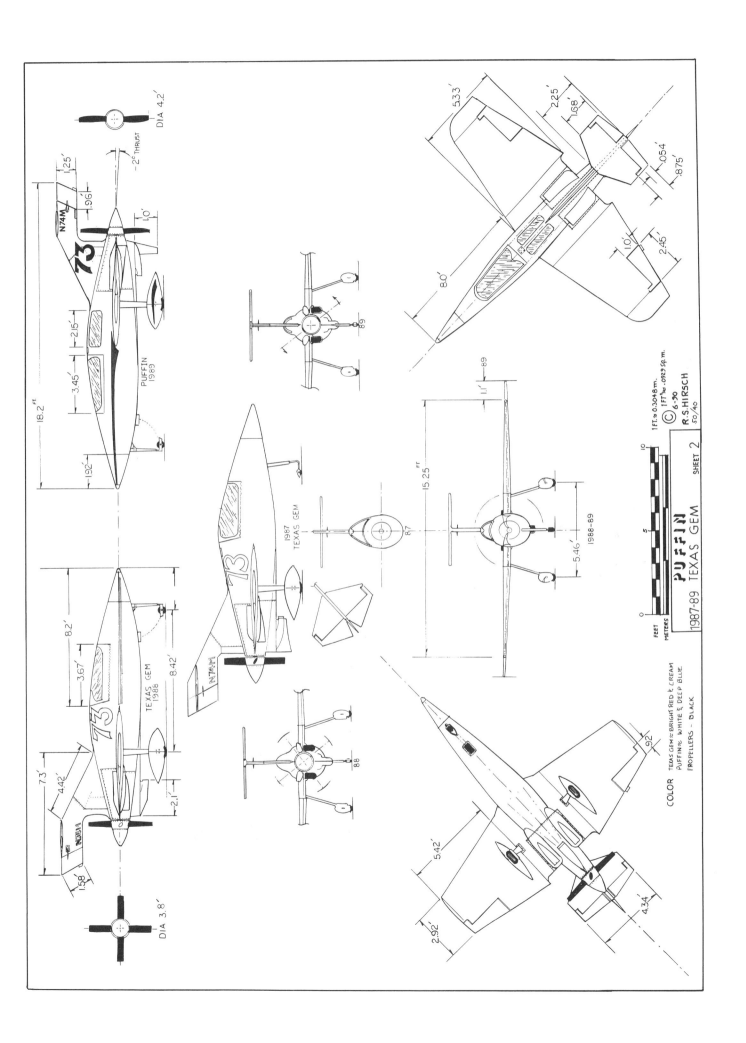

PUFFIN
1989

TEXAS GEM
1988

DIA 4.2'

DIA 3.8'

N74M

1987 TEXAS GEM

1988-89

COLOR TEXAS GEM ≈ BRIGHT RED & CREAM
PUFFIN ≈ WHITE & DEEP BLUE
PROPELLERS - BLACK

1 Ft. ≈ 0.3048 m.
1 Ft² ≈ .0929 sq.m.
© 6-90
R.S.HIRSCH
50/40

PUFFIN
1987-89 TEXAS GEM   SHEET 2

1970-74
"MOTHER HOLIDAY"
MARION BAKER

A NASA engineer, Marion Baker of Huron, OH, built this all-metal "Aquarius," (later "Mother Holiday") called the Baker 001 in 1970. It raced until 1976. In 1971 it placed 7th in Reno at 197.441 mph, and in 1973 it placed 9th fastest there at 214.712 mph. It was renumbered #20 and painted all white with red and blue trim. As #20 at the Sturgis, KY races on May 22-23 in 1971, it placed second at 213.270 mph.

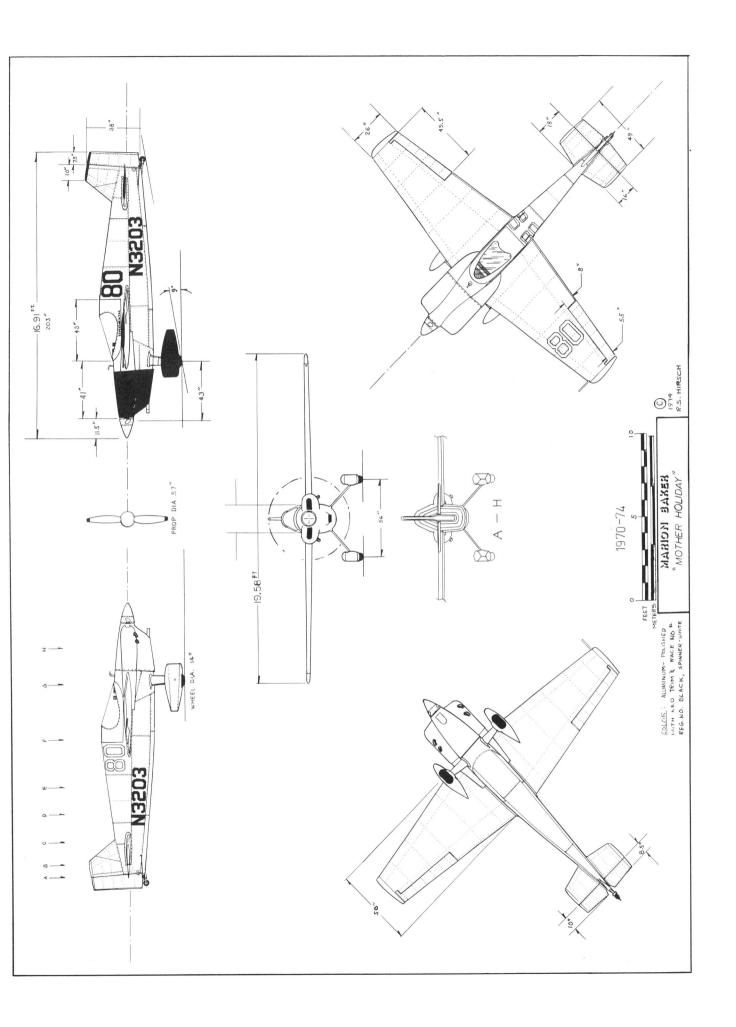

MARION BAKER
"MOTHER HOLIDAY"

1970-74

COLOR: ALUMINUM-POLISHED
WITH RED TRIM & RACE NO. #.
REG. NO. BLACK, SPINNER-WHITE

© 1974
R.S. HIRSCH

PROP DIA 57"

WHEEL DIA. 14"

16.91 FT.
203"

19.58 FT

N3203

80

A — H

CASSUTT
"BOO RAY"
MARION BAKER'S

"Boo Ray," a Cassutt, was slightly modified in 1977 with fuselage and cockpit changes. A new and tapered wing was added in 1984. "Pappy" Weaver worked on it as part of the crew.

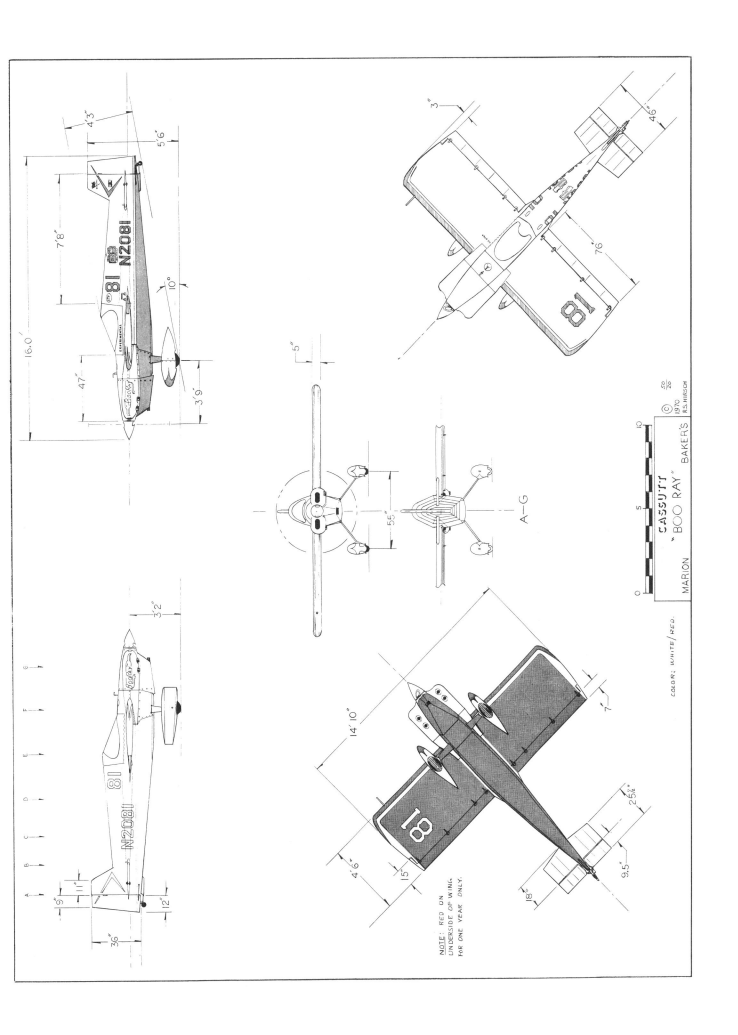

CASSUTT
"BOO RAY"

MARION   BAKER'S

COLOR: WHITE / RED.

NOTE: RED ON
UNDERSIDE OF WING.
FOR ONE YEAR ONLY.

A—G

© 50/20
1970
R.S. HIRSCH

1984
"Boo Ray"
Mod

"Boo Ray" was further modifed into this configuration in 1984. It was heavier and slower, and so did not do much racing until 1988.

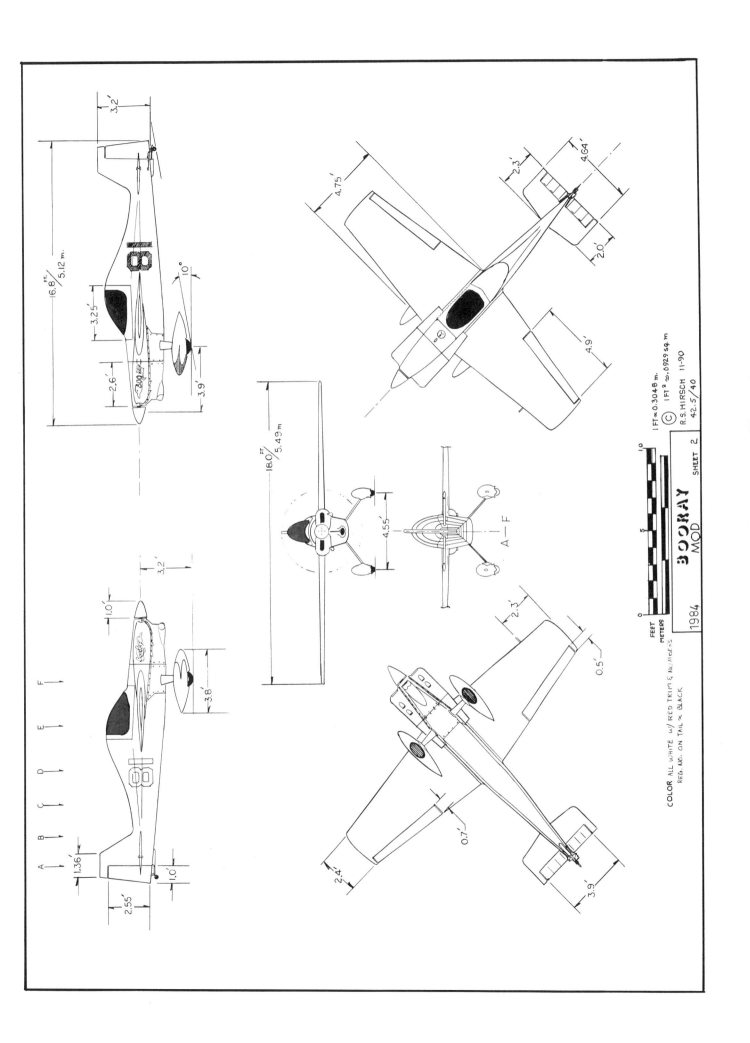

3.2'

16.8 FT. / 5.12 m.

3.25'

10°

2.6'

3.9'

3.2'

1.0'

3.8'

A
B
C
D
E
F

1.36'

2.55'

1.0'

18.0 FT. / 5.49 m

4.55'

A — F

4.75'

2.3'

4.64'

2.0'

4.9'

2.3'

0.5'

0.7'

2.4'

3.9'

COLOR ALL WHITE W/ RED TRIPLE E NUMBERS
REG. NO. ON TAIL & BLACK

1 FT ≈ 0.3048 m.
1 FT² ≈ .0929 sq. m
© R.S. HIRSCH 11-90
42.5/40

1984   BOORAY
MOD   SHEET 2

FEET
METERS
0   5   10

1988-89
"Boo Ray"
Mod

   "Boo Ray" showed up at Reno in 1988 modified again and was brought by Bill Berle (son of comedian Milton Berle) of Beverly Hills, CA. It was called the Baker-Wickman-Grove Cassutt but retained its name "Boo Ray." It qualified at 210.927 mph 15th down out of 23, and did 209.266 mph in heat C. It did not finish race 1-B. It flew almost too high around the courses. In August 1989 it was up for sale by Berle. It was then owned by Larry Jenson of Omaha, NE.

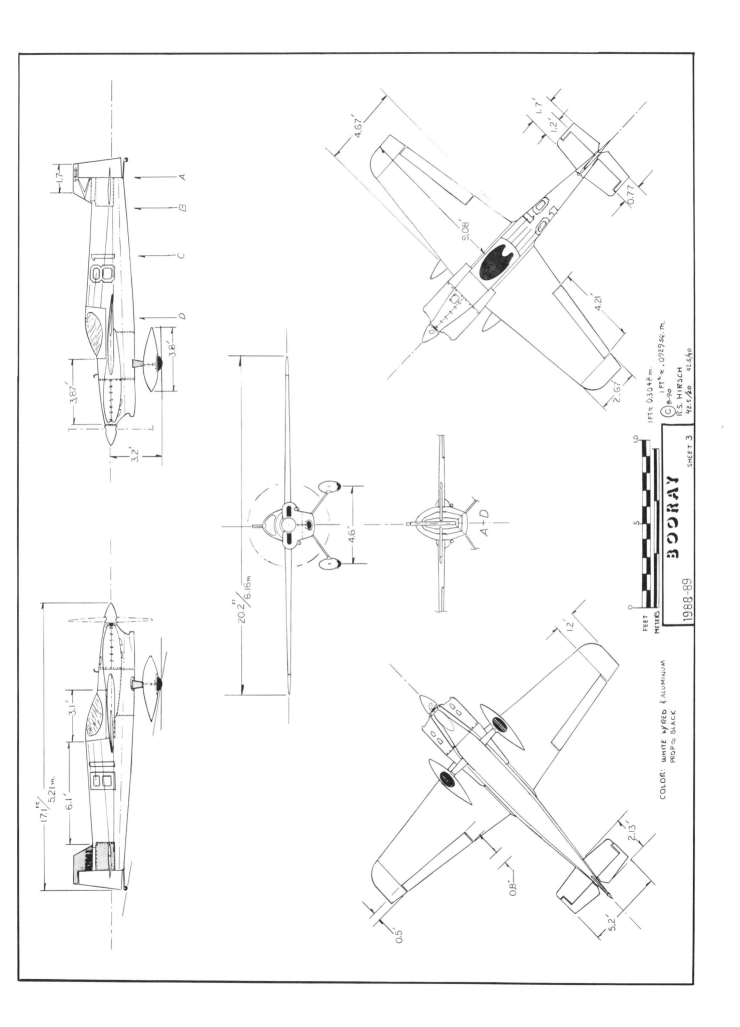

BOORAY

1988-89

SHEET 3

COLOR: WHITE W/RED & ALUMINUM
PROP ≃ BLACK

1 FT ≃ 0.3048 m.
1 FT² ≃ .0929 SQ.m.
© B-90
R.S. HIRSCH
42.5/20   42.5/40

1989-1996
"Pushy Galore"
Murmer Inc.

"Pushy Galore" is another Jim Miller designed pusher like "Pushy Cat," with modifications. It was built in six months and had its first flight in May 1989. It showed up in Reno just two years after "Pushy Cat." Bruce Bohanan was the owner/pilot. The NASA astronaut, Robert "Hoot" Gibson, also flew it to set a Class C-1-A altitude record. Bruce then followed suit with yet another record. "Pushy Galore" has attained 295 mph unofficially and has survived eight forced landings. The crew chief was Gary Hunter.

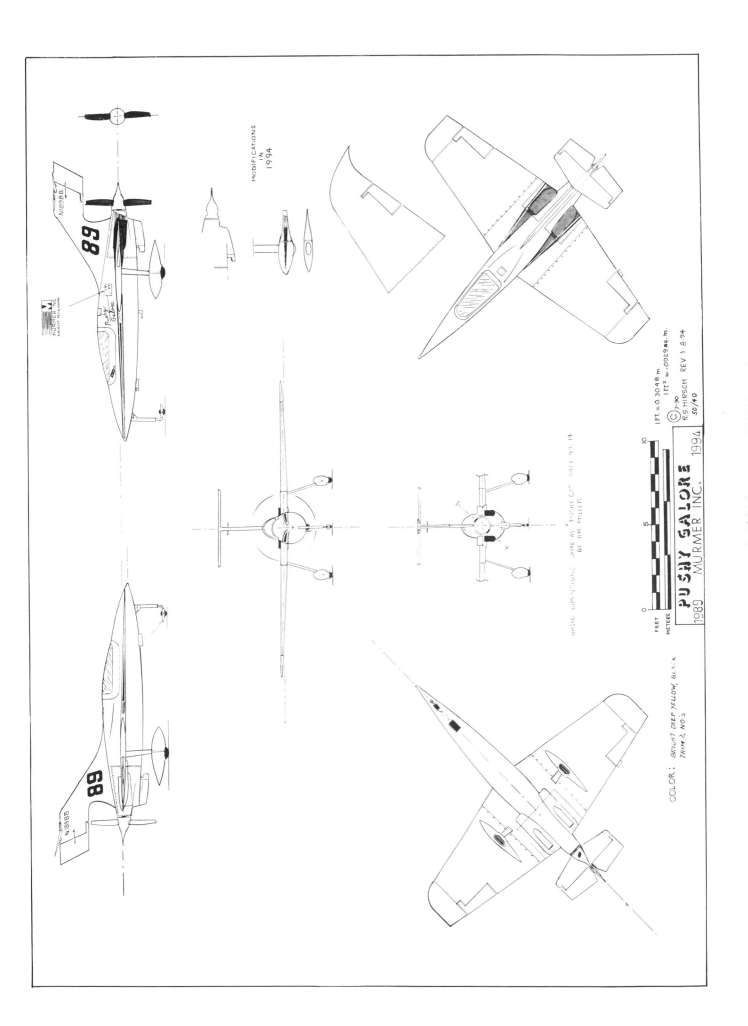

MODIFICATIONS IN 1994

BASIC DIMENSIONS SAME AS "PUSHY CAT" N/L NO. 14 BY JIM MILLER.

N189BB

COLOR: BRIGHT DEEP YELLOW, BLACK
TRIM & NO'S

1 FT. ≈ 0.3048 m
1 FT² ≈ .0929 sq. m.

© 7-90
R.S. HIRSCH REV 1 8-94
SO/40

PUSHY GALORE
1989   MURMER INC.   1994

FEET   0   5   10
METERS

1971-72
Tom Cooney
R-3

Thomas Cooney's R-3 is a thin lowered wing Cassutt he built in 1978. It didn't last long enough to race. In ferrying it to one of the races, and only ten miles from Cape May, his engine quit. Tom survived the landing unhurt. He eventually rebuilt the bright orange F-1 but didn't get to race it before he died of an illness.

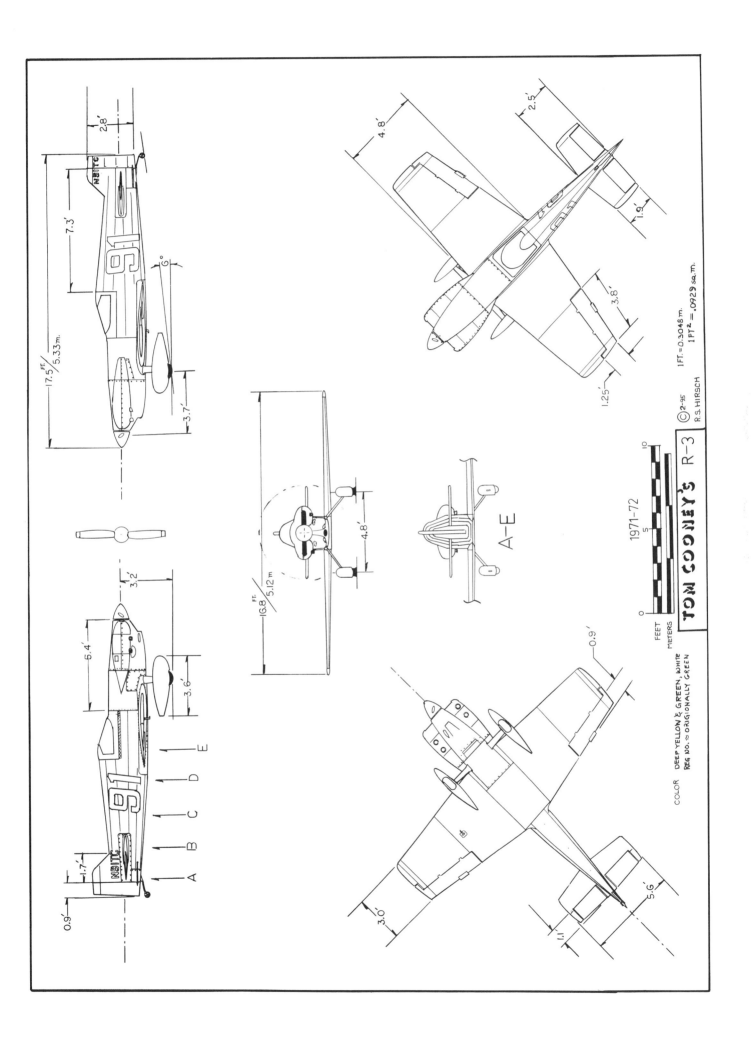

N911TC

191

6°

17.5 FT/5.33m.

7.3'

2.8'

3.7'

3.2'

5.4'

3.6'

1.7'

0.9'

N911TC

191

A B C D E

16.8 FT/5.12 m

4.8'

A-E

4.8'

2.5'

1.9'

3.8'

1.25'

0.9'

3.0'

1.1'

5.6'

COLOR DEEP YELLOW & GREEN, WHITE
REG. NO. ≈ ORIGIONALLY GREEN

1971-72

0   5   10
FEET
METERS

1 FT.= 0.3048 m.
1 FT²= .0929 sq.m.

© 2-95
R.S. HIRSCH

TOM COONEY'S R-3

1949-64
"Rivets
Bill Falck

It was a long 18 years between the time when Falck started his first racer and the day he won his first race. Here "Rivets" had been modified for 1949. It remained this way until about 1963-64 when it came with a "T" tail and new wheel covers.

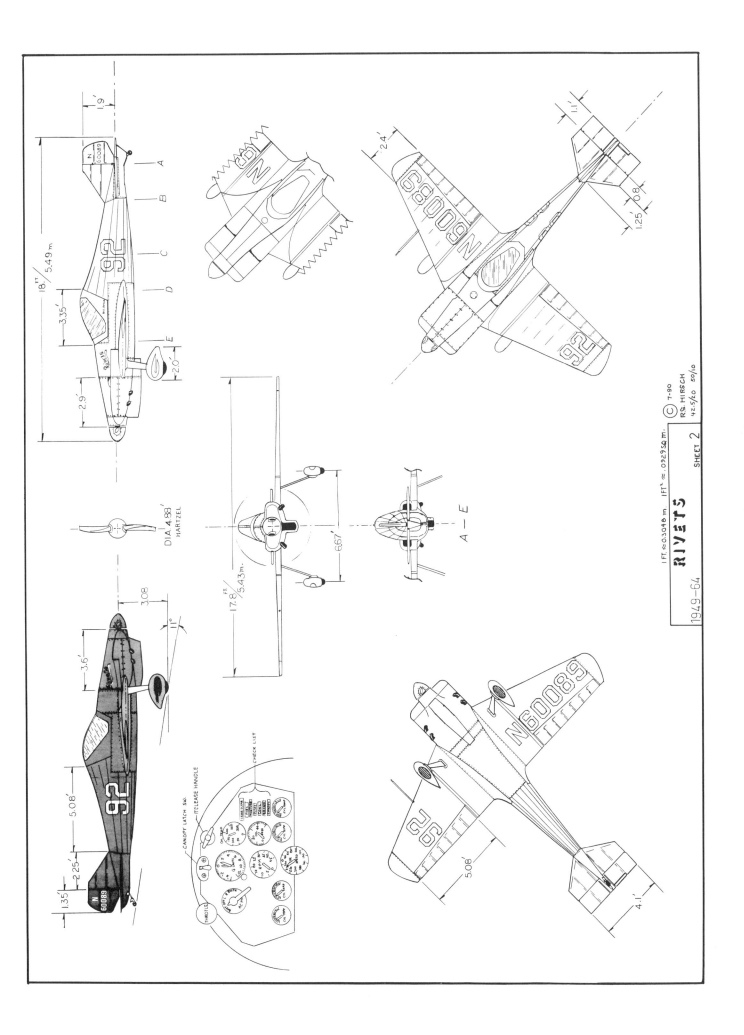

RIVETS

1949-64

1 FT. ≈ 0.3048 m. 1 FT² ≈ .0929 SQ m.

© 7-90
R.S. HIRSCH
42.5/60 50/10

SHEET 2

1965-77
"RIVETS"
BILL FALCK

"Rivets" with the new "T" tail underwent several minor aerodynamic changes in pursuit of greater speed. It first had rounded tips and later had square wingtips, and in 1973 Bill Falck recessed the ailerons somewhat and built curled down square wingtips. It remained much the same from 1965 until 1979 when it crashed, killing Bill. "Rivets" gave Bill first place no fewer than 50 times in all its races from 1949 to 1979, a good 28 years of racing. After about 10,000 hours of hard labor and over a 30-year period, it had the greatest winning streak of any racer. Its speed increased from 147 mph to 221 mph during that time.

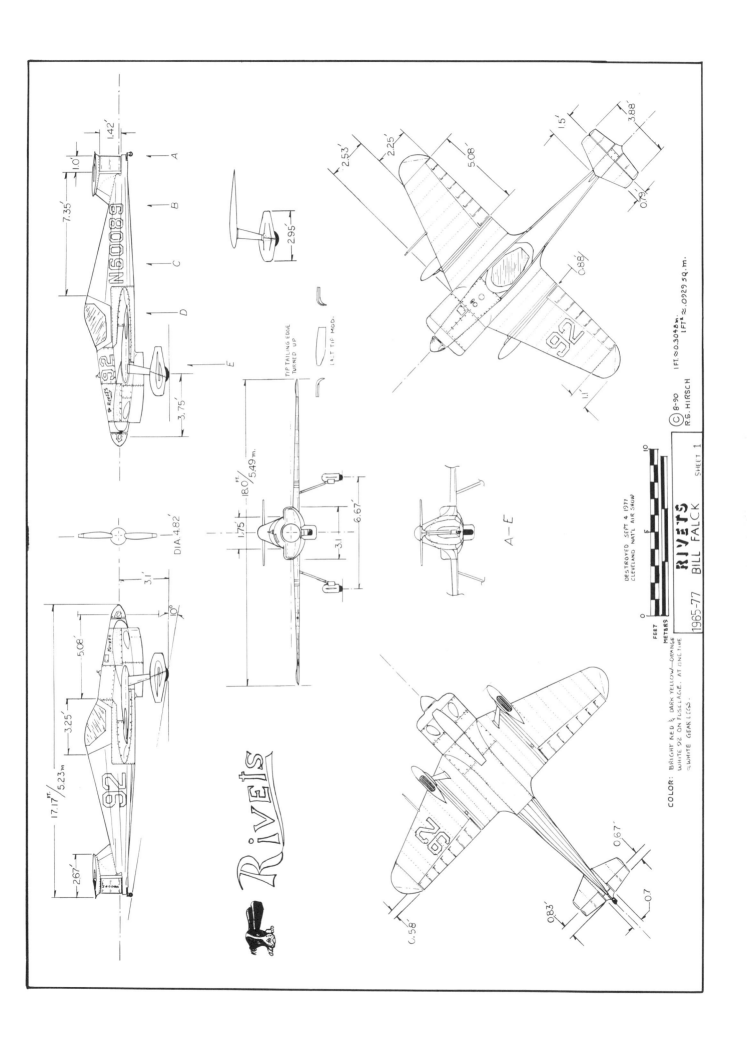

1.42'

1.0'

7.35'

N6008G

92

RIVETS

A

B

C

D

E

3.75'

TIP TRAILING EDGE
TURNED UP

I.R.T TIP MOD.

2.95'

2.53'

2.25'

5.08'

.15'

.388'

.79'

0.88'

92

1.1'

DIA 4.82'

3.1'

18.0'/5.49 m.

1.75'

6.67'

3.1'

A-E

10°

5.08'

3.25'

17.17'/5.23 m.

92

RIVETS

2.67'

RiveTs

0.58'

0.83'

92

0.67'

0.7

DESTROYED SEPT 4 1977
CLEVELAND NAT'L AIR SHOW

RIVETS

1965-77   BILL FALCK   SHEET 1

© 8-90
R.G. HIRSCH

1 FT. ≈ 0.3048 m.
1 FT² ≈ .0929 SQ. m.

FEET
METERS
0   5   10

COLOR: BRIGHT RED & DARK YELLOW–ORANGE
WHITE 92 ON FUSELAGE, AT ONE TIME
WHITE GEAR LEGS

1988-89
"POLY-DYNAMITE"
"HOOT" GIBSON

"Poly-Dynamite" was owned by Bruce Bohannon and Harold Peters and flown by astronaut Robert "Hoot" Gibson of Houston, TX. In 1989 he qualified at Reno at 197.365 mph and placed 5th in heat 1-C. After a couple of years of racing he had a mid-air accident and was grounded from racing by NASA. The plane was purchased by Eric Matheson in 1992, rebuilt and renamed "Yellow Peril." He qualified it at Reno at 194.27 that year. Dave Moss brought it to Reno in 1993 and qualified at 211.885 mph. In 1994 Dave placed 4th in the Gold race at 221.330 mph. The wing had been replaced with a Grove wing, and a Steve Hill carbon prop was installed. In 1995 the pilot was Matheson with Stu Luce as crew chief.

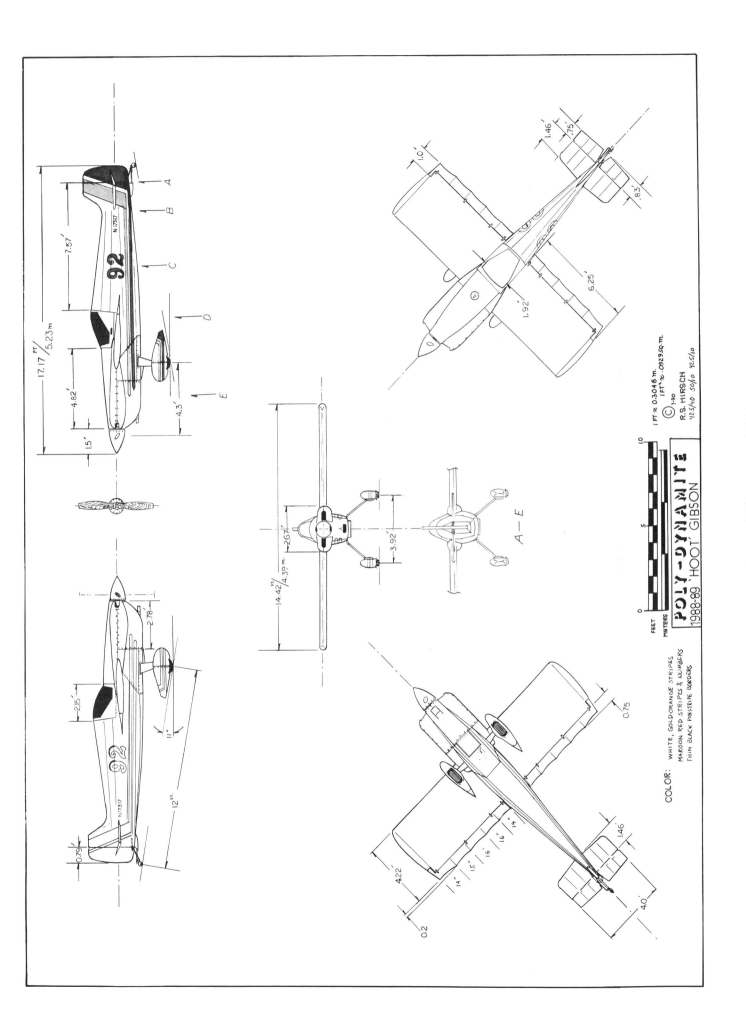

COLOR: WHITE, GOLD-ORANGE STRIPES
MAROON RED STRIPES & NUMBERS
THIN BLACK PINSTRIPE BORDERS

POLY-DYNAMITE
1988-89 'HOOT' GIBSON

FEET
METERS

1 FT ≈ 0.3048 m.
1 FT² ≈ .0929 sq. m.
© 7-90
R.S. HIRSCH
92.5/40 50/10 92.5/30

1970-72
"Rickey Rat"
Vince DeLuca

The first showing of this "Shoestring" K-10 was in 1970 at Reno. It was owned by Vincent DeLuca of Mira Leste, CA and flown by Tony Cooney. It was slightly heavier than #16. Vince flew it in 1971 and John Parker flew it in 1973 at Reno, Miramar and Point Mugu. It was called "Rickey Rat" and "Top Turkey." Bill Warwick raced it in 1976. In 1977 it showed up painted green with white trim and was flown by John Parker. In 1976 it was raced with a stock 0-200 without any mods or polish.

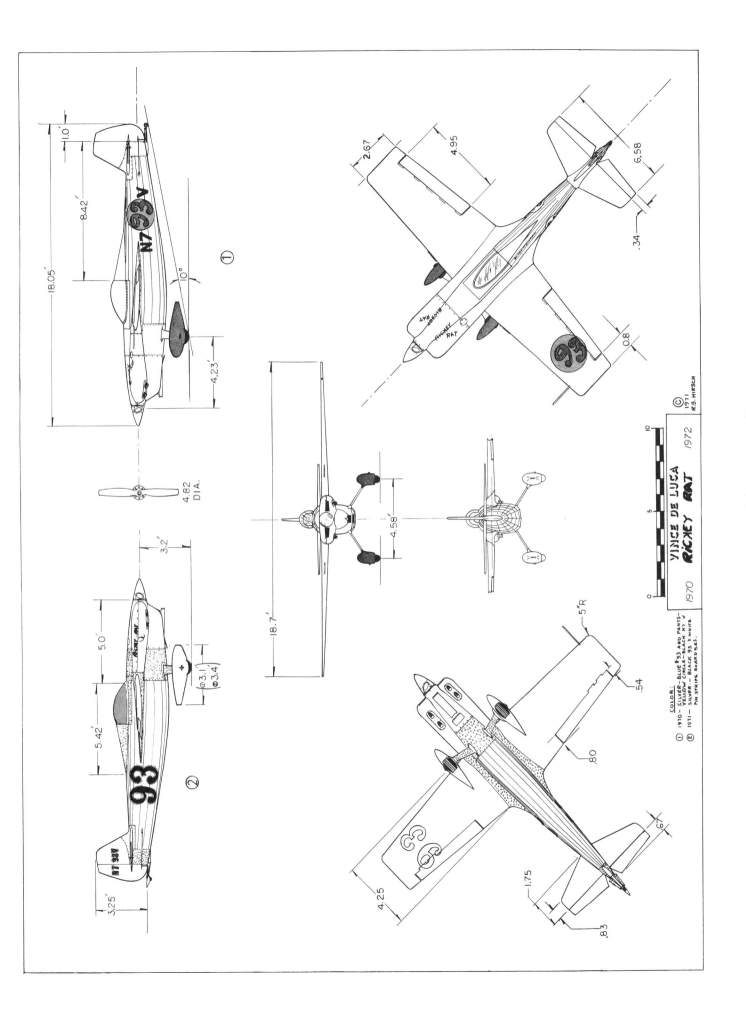

1.0'

8.42'

N7 93V

18.05'

10°

4.23'

①

4.82
DIA.

3.2'

5.0'

REMY RAT

5.42'

93

(∅3.1')
(∅3.4')

N7 93V

3.25'

②

2.67

4.95

6.58

.34

RICKEY
RAT

93

0.8

18.7'

4.58'

5"R

.54

.80

.67

4.25

1.75

.83

93

0 — 5 — 10

VINCE DE LUCA
RICKEY RAT

1970   1972

©
1971
R.S.HIRSCH

COLOR:
① 1970 - SILVER-BLUE #93 AND PANTS-
        YELLOW CIRCLE-BLACK N7 V
② 1971 - SILVER - BLACK 93 & WHITE
        FIN STRIPE BOARD EARS.

1990-94
"MARIAH"
GARY HUBLER

Gary Hubler of Valley Air Service in Caldwell, ID brought "Mariah" to Reno in 1990. It qualified at 221.011 mph and placed second in heat 2-B at 214.375 mph. In heat 1-A it only completed seven laps at a slow speed of 199.816 mph, and was last in the Gold race at 214.375. In 1991 at Reno, "Mariah" placed 7th in heat 2-A and in 1992 it was 9th down in qualifying at 223.736 mph, and finished 7th in the Gold at 215.437 mph. In 1994 it placed 3rd in the Gold race at 225.652 and 1st in heat 1-B at 226.617 mph. In 1995 it was 4th down in qualification at 232.234 and 3rd in heat 1-A at 234.269 mph. "Mariah" is a highly modified Cassutt III M built by James B. Hoover in 1971 and flown up to 1976 by Glenn Tuttle of Bountiful, UT, when it was put aside until 1990.

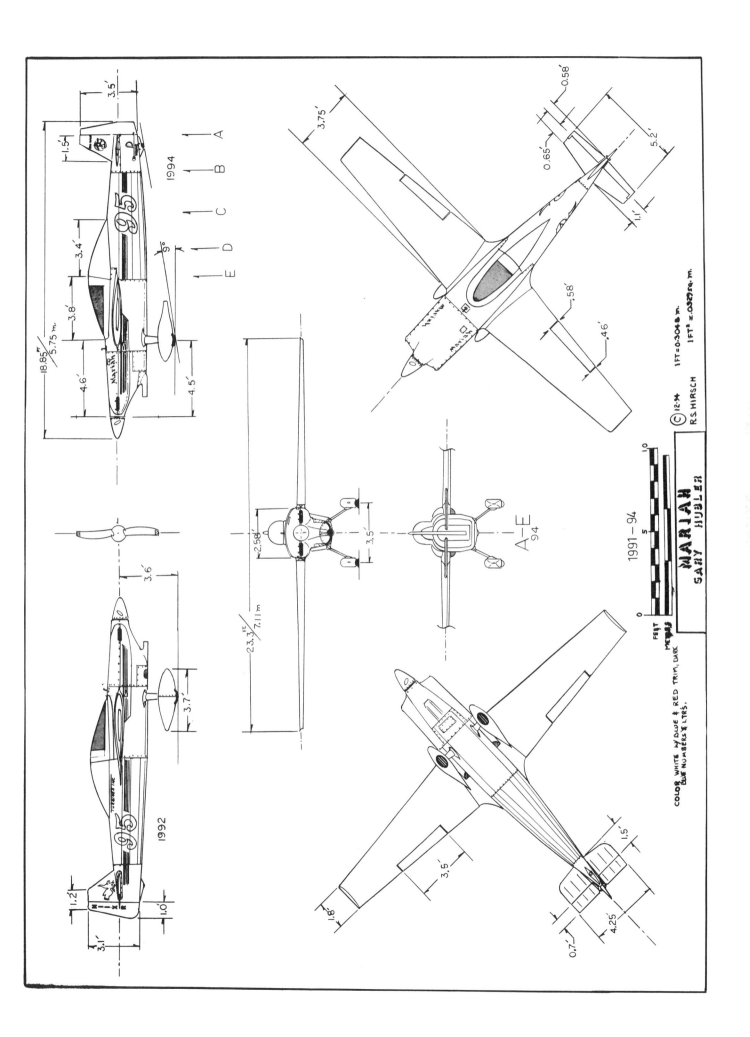

1994

1992

A B C D E

A—E
94

1991 – 94

MARIAH
GARY HUBLER

COLOR WHITE W/ BLUE & RED TRIM, DARK
BLUE NUMBERS & LTRS.

© 12.94
R.S. HIRSCH

1FT = 0.304 m.   1FT² = 0.0929 sq. m.

FEET
METERS

"Miss Dallas"
Denight
PDT Special

Leo Holiday of Dallas, TX owned the now-rebuilt "Miss Dallas" with a new red paint job and white numbers. Hewell "Nick" Jones of Augusta, GA was the pilot and finished 5th at Cleveland, OH and 7th at Frederick, MD in 1966. Its fastest speed was 197.8 mph. After the rebuild and some races it was sold to Dock Minges who placed second in the St. Louis Consolation races in 1967 and won the Cleveland Consolation race that same year.

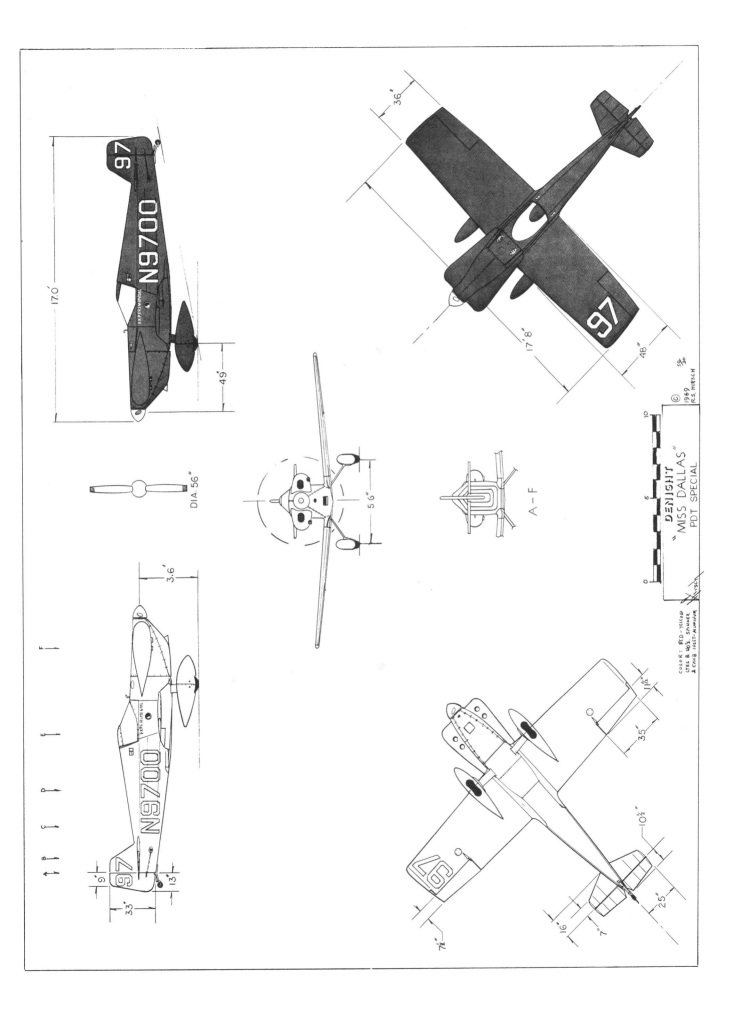

DENIGHT
"MISS DALLAS"
PDT SPECIAL

© 1969
R.S. HIRSCH

COLOR: RED-YELLOW
TIRES & WS. SPINNER
& CAB & DUCT-ALUMINUM

DIA. 56"

N9700

97

17.0'

49'

3.6'

5'6"

A - F

17'8"

48"

36"

33"
5'
13"

35'
11½"
10½"
25"
16"
7"
7¼"

"Ol' Blue"
Richard Minges

The "Miss Dallas" underwent once more a complete rebuild in 1970 and was designated M-30 and named "Ol' Blue" in 1971. The new owner/pilot was Richard Minges. In 1971 Thurman Rock of Santa Ana, CA owned it with Chuck Andrews as the pilot. John Bennett was the crew chief and Thurman sometimes piloted it. In 1987 it was piloted by Rocky Jones and did 215.059 mph. Jones had it up for sale for $18,000.

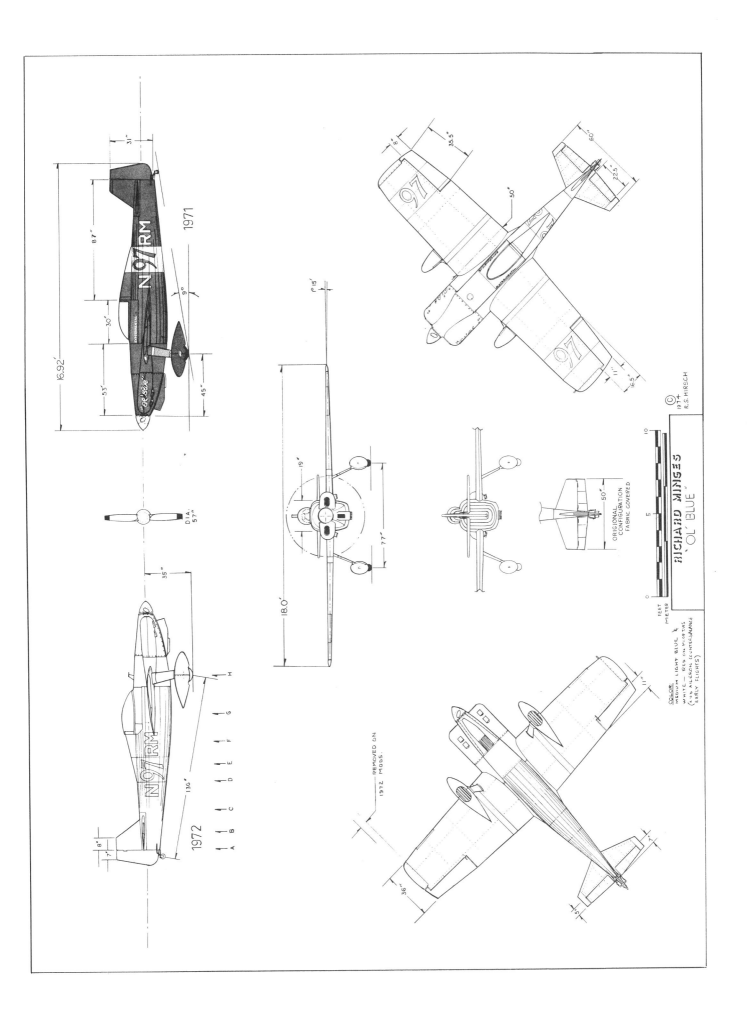

RICHARD MINGES
"OL' BLUE"

© 1974 R.S. HIRSCH

COLOR:
MEDIUM LIGHT BLUE &
WHITE — RED ON PLOTINS
(& b AILERON (COUNTERBALANCE
EARLY FLIGHTS)

ORIGIONAL
CONFIGURATION
FABRIC COVERED

REMOVED ON
1972 MODS.

1971

1972

DIA.
57"

16.92'

18.0'

FEET
METER

"MR. B"
HARVEY F. MACE
AL TREFETHEN

B.W. "Bud" Pedigo of Redding, CA was the owner/pilot of the Mace R-1 "Mr. B" built by Harvey Mace in 1966 for Al Trefethen of Lomita, CA. It first flew on March 4, 1966. It raced at Lancaster in 1966. Its design was started in 1965. At Reno in 1967 it qualified 8th down at 179.4 mph and won the Consolation race at 193.27 mph. The wings came from Terrill's "Poopsie Doll" and were modified to PRPA standards.

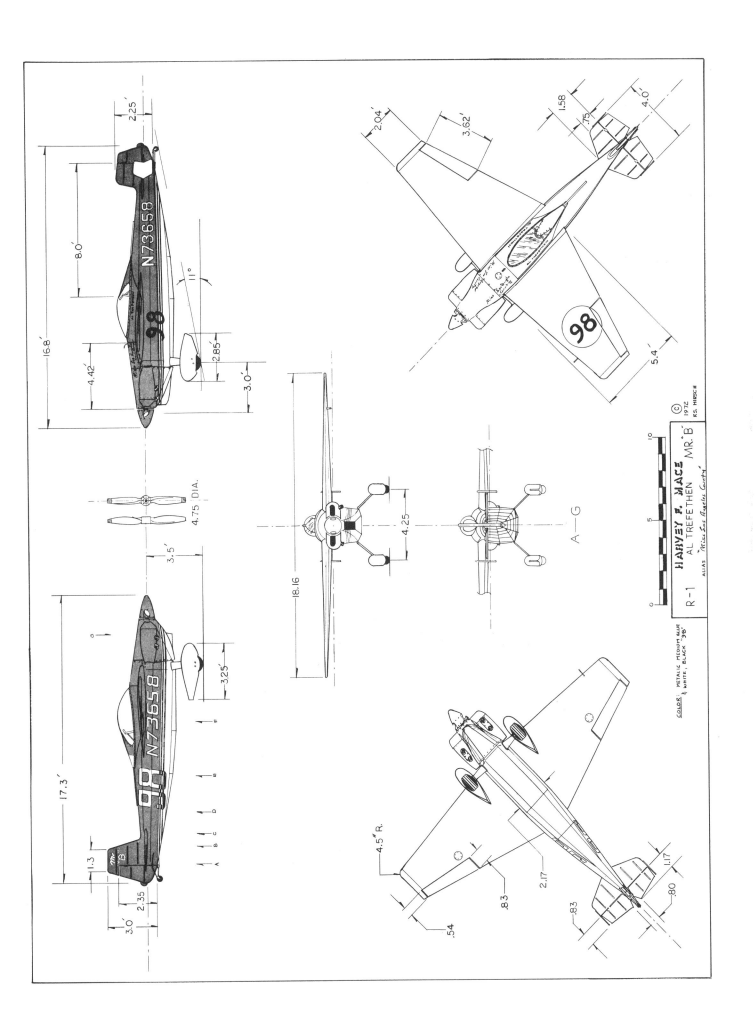

HARVEY R. MACE MR. "B"
AL TREFETHEN
ALIAS "Miss Los Angeles County"

COLOR: METALIC MEDIUM BLUE
& WHITE, BLACK "98"

R-1

© 1972
R.S. HIRSCH

"MR. B"
HARVEY MACE
BUD PEDIGO

Bud Pedigo had been racing "Mr. B" since 1968 but in 1970 he brought it to Reno highly modified where he won the Consolation race. The main difference was it went from a midwing to a low wing. It was raced in 1969 at Ft. Lauderdale, FL placing 4th in the Consolation race. Then in 1970, flying at 8,500 feet over Chester, CA, one half of the canopy came off ripping Bud's glasses off, cutting his eye. The wind impact pushed the headrest back three inches. He landed at Redding holding his hand over his cut eye. He had 32 stiches to his head, and then went on to Reno and raced. In the Consolation race his brakes failed and "Mr. B" didn't start.

160

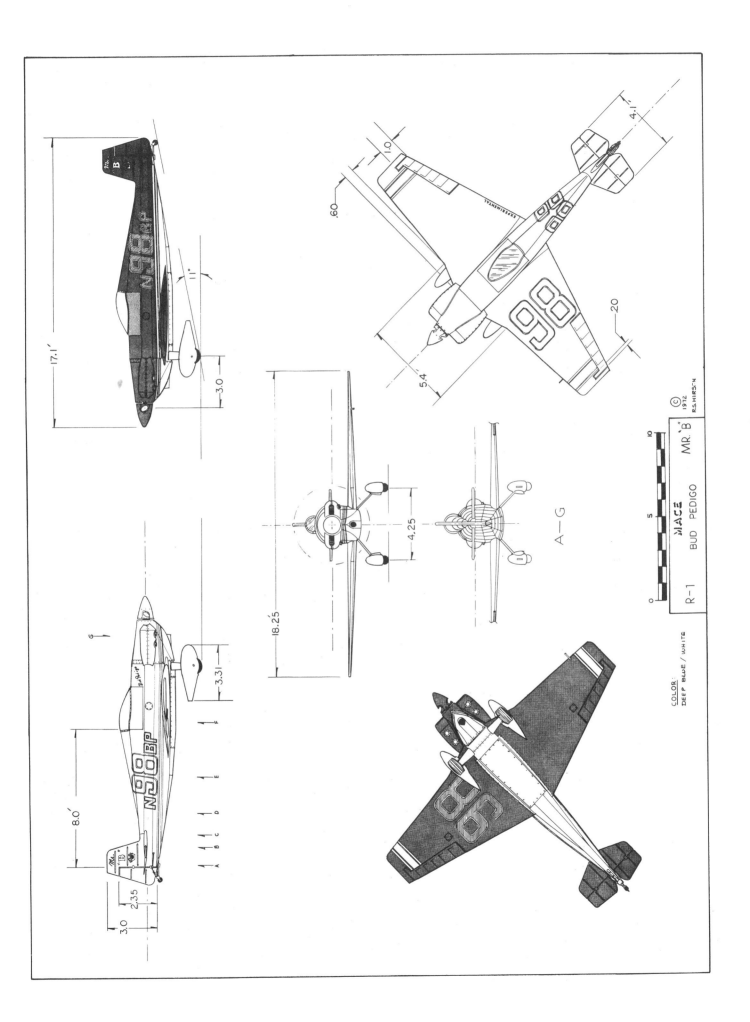

17.1'

11°

3.0

N98BP

B

G

8.0'

2.35

3.0

N98BP

3.31

A B C D E F

18.25'

4.25

A — G

1.0

.60

4.1'

5.4

.20

EXPERIMENTAL

98

98

COLOR:
DEEP BLUE / WHITE

MACE

BUD PEDIGO   MR. 'B'

R-1

0   5   10

©
1972
R.S. HIRSCH

1971
"MR. B"
BUD PEDIGO MOD 2

Bud Pedigo, a Cascade Camera Supply Store owner from Redding, CA, modified "Mr. B" again with a new tighter fitting, fiberglass cowl and air intake spinner. There also was a new paint job on it but it did not show at Reno that year. It did show in 1973 placing second behind Jim Stevenson's "Fang" at the Point Mugu Space Fair. In 1974 it was at Reno and did 215.139 mph for a qualifying speed, 9th down in a field of 20. Bud was 5th down in heat 1-A at 200.806 mph, and won the Silver race at 205.13 mph. 1975 was the last year "Mr. B" was active.

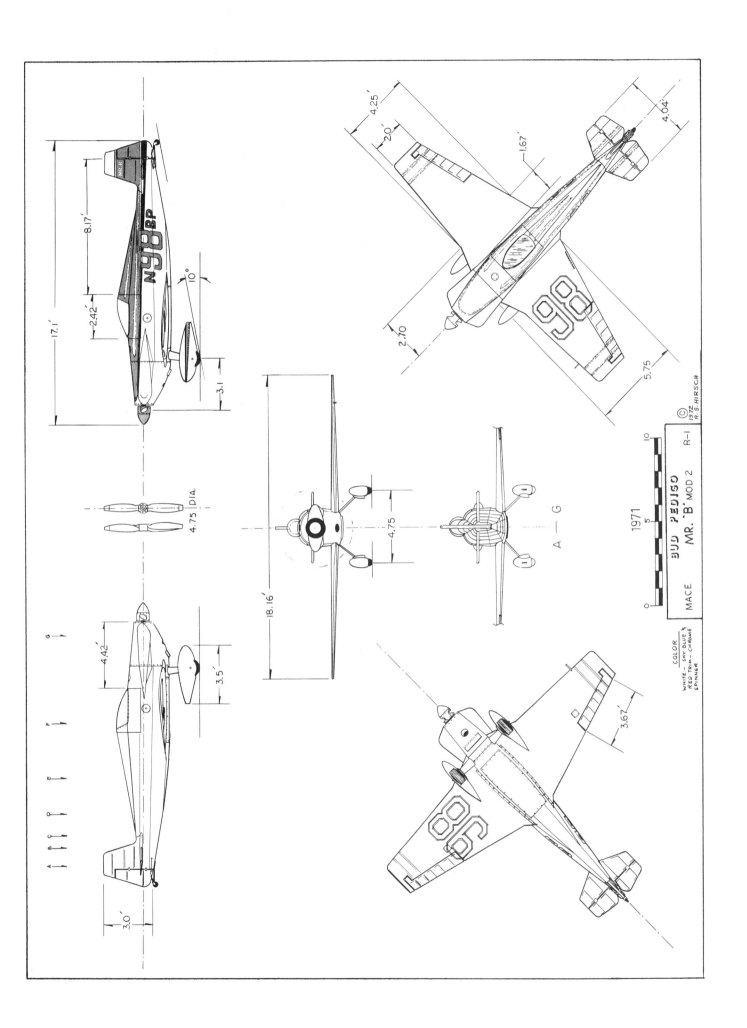

4.25'
2.0'
1.67'
4.04'
2.70
5.75'

17.1'
8.17'
2.42'
10°
3.1
N98BP
MR-B

4.75' DIA.

4.42'
3.5'
3.0'

18.16'

4.75'

A — G

3.67'

G
F
E
D
C
B
A

1971

MACE

BUD PEDIGO
MR. "B" MOD 2

R-1

© 1972
R.S.HIRSCH

0   5   10

COLOR
WHITE – SKY BLUE
RED TRIM – CHROME
SPINNER

1989-91
"FAST LANE EXIT"
DAVE MORSS

In 1989 "Crazy" Dave Morss of San Carlos, CA was owner/pilot of "Fast Lane Exit." In 1986 Morss owned and entered at Reno a Cassutt III M which was yellow with red trim and number 66 named "Video Cassutt" which qualified at 179.653 mph. This single wheel version of "Fast Lane Exit" qualified relatively fast and did fairly well in the heat races. It remained in the mono wheel configuration until 1991.

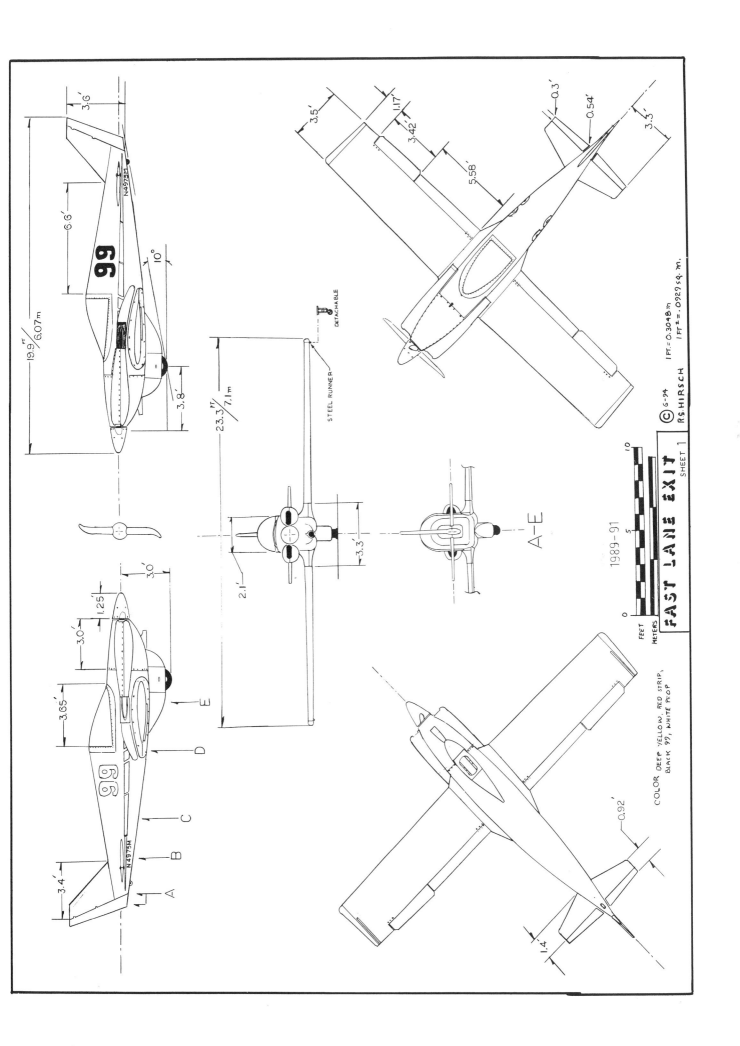

N4975M

99

3.6'

6.6'

19.9' / 6.07 m

10°

3.8'

23.3' / 7.1 m

STEEL RUNNER

DETACHABLE

2.1'

3.3'

A-E

3.0'

1.25'

3.0'

3.65'

N4975M

3.4'

99

A B C D E

3.5'

1.17

3.42

5.58

0.3'

0.54

3.3'

0.92

1.4

1989-91

COLOR DEEP YELLOW, RED STRIP,
BLACK 99, WHITE PROP

FEET

METERS

© G-94
R.S.HIRSCH

FAST LANE EXIT
SHEET 1

1FT.=0.3048m
1FT²=.0929 SQ. M.

0   5   10

"FAST LANE EXIT"
DAVE MORSS

In 1993 Dave Morss' "Fast lane Exit" came with a standard two wheels and tail wheel. It used either a 3-blade or a 2-blade propeller trying to find the right balance. It raced in 1993 and 1994 but didn't show in 1995. In 1993 it qualified at a slow 176.065 mph, and placed 5th in the Bronze race at 180.662 mph. It showed up at Reno in 1994 but did not qualify.

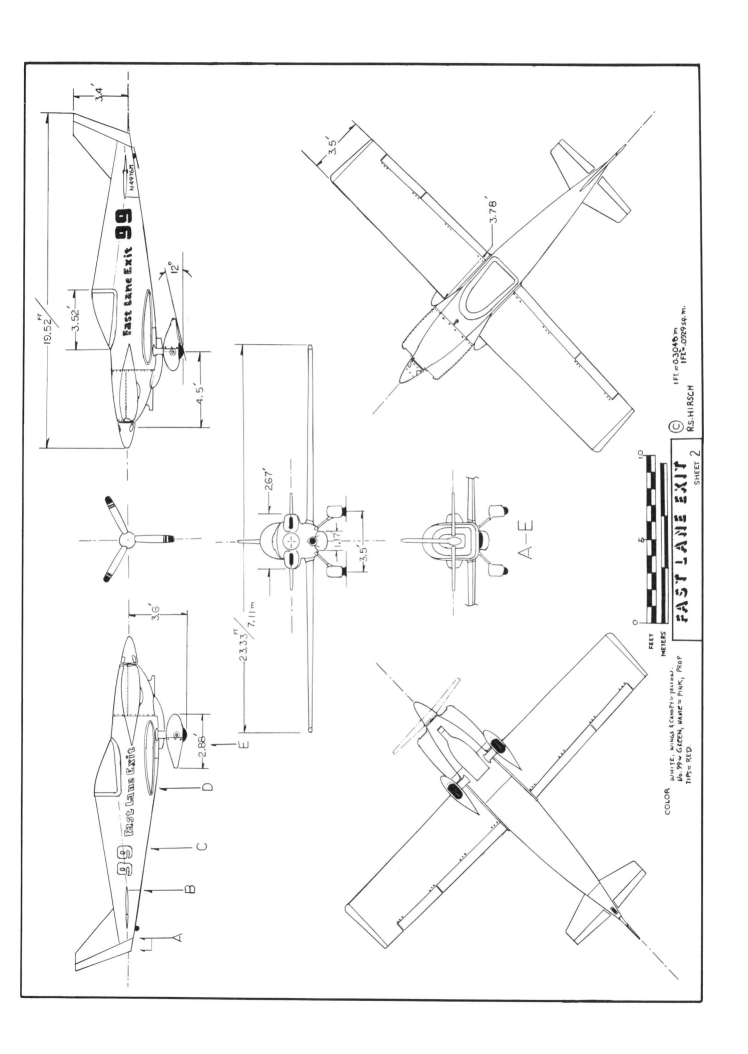

FAST LANE EXIT
SHEET 2

COLOR WHITE, WINGS & CANOPY~YELLOW,
No. 99~ GREEN, NAME~ PINK, PROP
TIPS~ RED

1 FT.=0.3048 m
1 FT²=.0929 SQ.m.
© R.S.HIRSCH

MORE AIRCRAFT PHOTOS

No. 9 "Cyclone" N-1329 in 1967 by Fred Wofford of Tahoe City, CA. It later became "Gold Dust" and raced in 1969 at Reno only. It placed 4th but cut a pylon and was moved back to 5th.

This No. 7 was No. 3 "Cosmic Wind" and raced in the mid 1960s and 1970s at Reno and Cleveland. "Little Toni" was brought out of storage and flown by Roy Berry.

This Cassutt N-101M "One More Time" was built in 1987 and flown by Vince Kirol of Jackson, NY.

This Cassutt III M (N-25VS) named "Frenzy" was raced in 1995 by David Hoover of Foster City, CA. It placed 4th in the Silver race at Reno. It had a new wing in 1996.

MORE AIRCRAFT PHOTOS

This Cassutt III M (N-8155) "Sue" came came to Reno in 1992-95. I.B. Hansen of Arrada, CO was the pilot/owner.

No. 17, the Cassutt "Annie" (N45889), was brought to Reno in 1995 by Carl J. Swanson, Jr. of Montgomery, TX. It has been around for some time — it qualified in 1988 at 211 mph.

Still Racing

This Cassutt III M "Black Majic" (N-13EL) was brought to Reno from 1974 through 1984 by Gary Hubler of Caldwell, ID. It also was flown by a Mr. Janson.

Don Beck of Tahoe-Vista, CA had this Cassutt "Gnat" (N-5381) at Reno but in 1986-87 Earol Johnstad of Berlin, Germany had it and named it "Slapknow."

now #40 MISS USA
N5381

MORE AIRCRAFT PHOTOS

This view was taken at Reno in 1990 of the Cassutt N-20HI "Super Chick" (also "Trick Chick" and "Spooky") owned by Tom Wrolstad and Harry Volpe.

This No. 7 "Wise Owl" is modified from Vince DeLuca's "Little Quickie" No. 71. It later was purchased by Ray Cote and became No. 4 "Alley Cat." This aircraft came to Reno in the late 1970s and early 1980s.

No. 24ML, the Shoestring K-10 "Spud Runner" by Monroe Lycth, Jr. in 1972, was renamed "No Big Thing" by Patrick Pediker in 1973. Greg Paster was also involved with this racer, as was Dave Morss in 1987.

There are many of these midget racers and race types that are not mentioned here simply because there is not enough room to handle all of them. Almost all of the various configurations are covered in the drawings — that is, up to 1995.

It is hoped that what is here has provided insight to this great sport. Many, including this author, feel that the sport, as exciting as it already is, could be enhanced by creating another class with a small step upward in power and components, but keeping with the same general principles of the Formula One racers. These changes, along with using a slightly larger course, such as the T-6 course, could allow speeds approaching the P-51 and would be very interesting to watch.